T0177402

Game Design Deep Dive

Game Design Deep Dive

Horror

Joshua Bycer

CRC Press
Taylor & Francis Group
Boca Raton   London   New York

CRC Press is an imprint of the
Taylor & Francis Group, an **informa** business

First edition published 2022
by CRC Press
6000 Broken Sound Parkway NW, Suite 300, Boca Raton, FL 33487-2742

and by CRC Press
2 Park Square, Milton Park, Abingdon, Oxon, OX14 4RN

ISBN: 978-1-032-05806-1 (hbk)
ISBN: 978-0-367-72174-9 (pbk)
ISBN: 978-1-003-19925-0 (ebk)

DOI: 10.1201/9781003199250

Typeset in Minion
by codeMantra

Contents

Preface

With each book I have written, I feel like I am getting into a groove with how to organize the *Game Design Deep Dive* series. This is good, because we are now getting into one of the hardest genres in my opinion to talk about: horror.

I have had a strange relationship with horror throughout my life. As a child, I was terrified of just about everything and had a nightlight for the longest time. Games, TV, movies, it did not matter, I could not take it growing up. It was not until two leg surgeries and growing up that horror did not bother me anymore. Over the last 17 years, I have played horror from all corners of the industry and caught up on many of the most popular horror franchises I missed out. Today, I have yet to play one game that has managed to scare me enough to stop me from playing it.

What I am going to be discussing in this book can be applied to not only videogames but other mediums as well, and that is the beauty of horror. There is something universal and primal about fear that I am going to examine in this book. Being able to create a tense or memorable atmosphere extends beyond horror and knowing the psychology behind it will help. As always, I am interested in what you think of each of my works and feel free to reach out with my contact information under the "Social Media Contact" section.

Social Media Contact

Email: Josh@game-wisdom.com

My YouTube channel where I post daily design videos and developer interview: youtube.com/c/game-wisdom

Main site: Game-Wisdom.com

My Twitter: Twitter.com/GWBycer

Additional Books

If you enjoyed this entry and want to learn more about design, you can read my other works:

- **20 Essential Games to Study:** A high level look at 20 unique games that are worth studying their design to be inspired by or for a historical look at the game industry.
- **Game Design Deep Dive: Platformers:** The first entry in the *Game Design Deep Dive* series focusing on 2D and 3D platformer design, and a top-to-bottom discussion of the history, mechanics, and design of the game industry's most recognizable and long-lasting genre.
- **Game Design Deep Dive: Roguelikes:** The second entry in the *Game Design Deep Dive* series focusing on the rise and design of roguelike games. A look back at how the genre started, what makes the design unique, and an across-the-board discussion on how it has become the basis for new designs by modern developers.

Acknowledgments

For each one of my books, I run a donation incentive for people to be acknowledged. Here are the people who helped support me while I was writing *Game Design Deep Dive: Horror*:

Michael Berthaud
D.S
Thorn Falconeye
Adriaan Jansen
Jonathan Ku
Robert Leach
Aron Linde
Josh Mull
Mjmbk
Rey Obomsawin
Onslaught
David Pittman
Puppy Games

Author

Joshua Bycer is a Game Design Critic with more than 8 years of experience critically analyzing game design and the industry itself. In that time, through Game-Wisdom, he has interviewed hundreds of game developers and members of the industry about what it means to design video games. He also strives to raise awareness about the importance of studying game design by giving lectures and presentations; his first book was titled *20 Essential Games to Study*. He continues to work on books in the *Game Design Deep Dive* series.

The Goal of *Game Design Deep Dive: Horror*

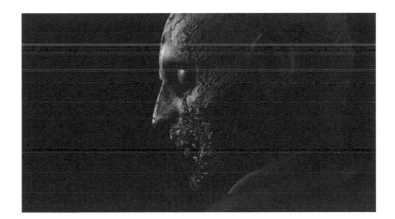

Figure 1.1

One of the most iconic moments from *Resident Evil* with the introduction of the first zombie and a good introduction for this book.

For this entry in the *Game Design Deep Dive* series, I turn to what may be the hardest one to write about. Horror isn't the same kind of genre as the other entries: There are no predefined **mechanics**, and just about every kind of gameplay **system** could be applied to horror, and I have seen **indie** developers attempt just that over the 2010s (Figure 1.1).

DOI: 10.1201/9781003199250-1

Instead, horror is about a certain kind of philosophy that many developers try to achieve, but few do. My purpose here is not to give you a mechanical breakdown of every possible variation of horror, as that would be impossible. I am going to be discussing the psychological levers you need to pull if you want to generate terror in your consumer. By studying both major and minor examples of horror, you can begin to see the common threads of titles that either work or do not. Creating horror through gameplay is about understanding what tension is and how to manipulate it through atmosphere and design. Learning to control tension can be applied to any game where you want to quickly change the mood and there are plenty of ways of doing that.

If you are a general consumer of the game industry, you may know some of the major names that have appeared in the last 30 years, but as with **roguelikes** in the second part of this series, a lot of the growth from the genre has come from indie developers experimenting with their own style and storytelling.

Let us begin with the first challenge: tracing the origins of horror in the game industry.

2

The Pre-survival Horror Period

Figure 2.1

Very few horror properties retained their horror when brought to consoles and arcades in the 1980s and 1990s.

2.1 The Monster Mashup

Monster iconography has been used across all entertainment mediums for decades. Part of the issue when it comes to defining the start of horror is that

DOI: 10.1201/9781003199250-2

3

many games used horror monsters and properties but were not really focused on scaring the **player**. I will discuss more on defining what horror is in Chapters 4 and 5.

Many franchises from the 1980s and onward used popular **IPs** as the basis for videogames. Popular films like *A Nightmare on Elm Street, Jaws, Friday the 13th, Alien,* and more had videogame adaptations (Figure 2.1). Despite being based on scary properties, these games were drastically toned down for several reasons. The limitations on technology at the time prevented games from being perfect retellings of the films. The stories were changed to allow for more gameplay elements which gave more power to the players. In the 1980s and into the 1990s, videogame content was rigorously controlled by the parent company of respective platforms.

During Nintendo's control over the console market, they explicitly banned graphic or religious imagery from games on the Nintendo Entertainment System (or more commonly referred to as the NES) and the Famicom, which was the Japanese version of the console. Nintendo's demand on developers would eventually lead to the great market war between Sega and Nintendo, with Sega being far more lenient in terms of content.

There were many games released that had monster enemies and even some that let players control monsters that were more about action than horror. Both the NES and Sega Genesis had breakout horror-adjacent franchises.

Konami became famous for both console and arcade games and was one of the premiere developers for a time. In 1986, they released the game *Vampire Killer* which would then be translated and released in the United States under the name *Castlevania*. The *Castlevania* franchise followed the Belmont family who were the only ones who could defeat Dracula. Each game featured impressive music and a litany of horror icons like werewolves, Frankenstein's monster, and the Grim Reaper. The series would span multiple games, platforms, and changing genres multiple times.

Famously, one of the iconic weapons in the game had to be changed. The Holy Cross was originally conceived to be used as a boomerang-type weapon. Nintendo demanded that Konami changed it to not spark controversy with religious groups. It was changed to be a four-sided weapon and just called a boomerang and has been featured in multiple games.

Originally released in arcades and then **ported** to consoles, the *Splatterhouse* franchise by Namco was one of the first games to feature full-on gore in them and mirrored the splatter films released (Figure 2.2). The first game was released in arcades in 1988, and the following two were released on home consoles. The series starred Rick who had to save his girlfriend Jennifer from demons and monsters while wearing the "terror mask" that looked a lot like the hockey mask from the *Friday the 13th* films. Even though the game was full of disturbing enemy designs, this was not a game about the player being scared and is a good example of the concept of the "power fantasy" that I will return to in Chapter 6. The series would go on to have one 3D sequel for the PlayStation 3 and Xbox 360 released in 2010, but turmoil during development and low sales would end it there.

2. The Pre-survival Horror Period

Figure 2.2

Splatterhouse and games like it were about fighting monsters and overcoming them as part of a power fantasy.

As a strange coincidence, both *Castlevania* and *Splatterhouse* would also get kid-friendly spin off games for the NES: *Kid Dracula* and *Splatterhouse Wanpaku Graffiti* released in 1990 and 1989, respectively. Both games replaced the serious stories with cartoon antics.

When most fans and consumers discuss the biggest names of horror in the game industry, there are four games that I will be talking about that each left a mark when it came to establishing and growing the horror genre.

3

The Rise of Survival Horror

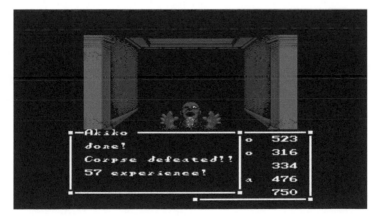

Figure 3.1

Sweet Home would go on to inspire *Resident Evil*, despite being completely different in terms of design and structure.

DOI: 10.1201/9781003199250-3

3.1 *Sweet Home*

In 1989, Capcom released the game *Sweet Home* for the Famicom and is considered by many to be the first survival horror game ever made (Figure 3.1). Named after the popular Japanese film, the story followed a five-person film crew who arrived at an old mansion to find Frescos and ended up being trapped by a vengeful ghost. To escape, players had to use the team and their unique abilities and gear to solve puzzles, fight monsters, and avoid deadly traps. The player was free to group the characters into different teams to explore the mansion, and each one started with an item needed to solve puzzles. Like a roguelike, the game featured a **permadeath** system that if a character was killed, they were removed from the rest of the play.

Unlike the other games in this chapter, *Sweet Home* was played as a **role-playing game** (or RPG). Exploring the mansion took place from a **top-down** perspective. When the player runs into an enemy, the game would shift into a **first-person** perspective – which was a popular style for RPGs to fight the enemies in at the time. Depending on how many characters were still alive at the end would determine what ending the player received.

For the time of its release, *Sweet Home* was one of the deepest games. The multi-party system that allowed players to have characters team up or break away was original. Animated cutscenes were used rarely for storytelling during that era, which *Sweet Home* used. This would also be one of the first examples of a game making use of **quick time events** (or QTEs) that failing would lead to a character possibly dying.

Sweet Home would go on to define many of the elements that make up survival horror that I will elaborate on in Section 4.2 and was cited as a major inspiration for *Resident Evil* that will be discussed in Section 3.3. The gameplay of battling fearsome monsters with limited resources has been the foundation for many horror games. Challenging the player to solve puzzles was a major element that has been featured in each series in this chapter.

Despite the popularity and renown surrounding it, *Sweet Home* was never officially translated and released outside of Japan. Theories online suggest that the game's violent imagery clashed with Nintendo's focus on family-friendly content. Another theory was that RPGs did not achieve widespread popularity yet. In the early 2000s, the **ROM** for *Sweet Home* was cracked and uploaded to the internet with a fan-made translation. This is the only way at the time of writing this book that it is possible to play a translated version of the game even though possessing cracked ROMs is considered illegal.

3.2 *Alone in the Dark*

Part of the confusion about the origins of horror in the videogame industry is that while *Sweet Home* was technically the first, it did not achieve success outside of Japan and most audiences did not hear about it at the time of release. Instead,

Figure 3.2

Alone in the Dark would become the foundation for survival horror with its use of real-time combat, exploration, and puzzle solving.

Alone in the Dark had a further reach and is the game people often credited as the start of survival horror (Figure 3.2).

Created by Frédérick Raynal and Infogrames, the first game was released in 1992 for MS-DOS with console releases a few years later. The story involved playing as one of two characters who had to investigate a mysterious death at Derceto Manor. The two characters, Edward Carnby and Emily Hartwood, played the same way, with Edward becoming the series' main protagonist for future games.

At a **GDC** talk, Frédérick discussed the inspiration for the gameplay of *Alone in the Dark*. The concept was to take the puzzle solving and critical thinking used in an adventure game and combine it with the player having to deal with threats that could kill them like an action game. Players could see this with how the **core gameplay loop** worked. Exploring the manor was done in real time, with the ability to equip or use items from the inventory screen. Interacting required choosing a verb from the menu that would then be assigned to the game's "action" button.

When attacked, players could fight off monsters with their fists and found weapons. While there were guns, they were hard to use and there was limited ammo. Enemy design was a big part of the game and a topic I will discuss more in Section 6.3. There were three kinds of enemies in the game. Low-level zombies and monsters that the player had to fight off or avoid best they could. Larger enemies that were tied to specific puzzles or obstacles that required a specific item or solution to deal with. Finally, there were enemies that could not be killed, and the player must avoid them or be killed instantly.

Each floor of the manor had puzzles that needed to be solved and is the one area where *Alone in the Dark* is the most dated in terms of design. The game was released during the golden age of adventure game design and embodied the often-confusing puzzle logic that was a part of the genre. Even though there were clues and hints to find, the logic needed to connect them to a puzzle was often

Figure 3.3

Despite the early 3D graphics, *Alone in the Dark* tried to create tension with is cutscenes and mood.

hard to follow. To add to the danger, the game featured many death traps that unknowing players could trigger ending their game immediately.

From a technology standpoint, *Alone in the Dark* was ahead of its time as one of the first fully 3D games with all the characters made up of polygons. Due to how the game used 3D characters with 2D backgrounds, it was necessary to lock the camera angles to fixed perspectives which also added to the tension of not knowing what was behind a corner (Figure 3.3). When the player moved their character, it was in relation to the positioning and direction of the model instead of where the camera was pointing. To change direction, they would have to push the left or right arrows to rotate the model and then press up to have them walk forward. This kind of system would become referred to as "tank-like controls" and would be a mainstay of horror games until 2005.

The use of fixed camera angles and the control scheme would be just one of several areas where *Alone in the Dark* would go on to cement the foundation of survival horror gameplay. When I discuss the basics of horror design in the game industry, this is the game and series that its DNA can be seen in future titles, including our next two examples in this chapter. *Alone in the Dark* as a franchise would go on to release four main games and two reboots/spin-offs, and had two movies made about it. At the time of writing this book, the poor reception of the last two games, and Frédérick no longer having the rights to work on it, has put an end to the series.

3.3 *Resident Evil*

If *Sweet Home* was the start of horror and *Alone in the Dark* was the progenitor, then *Resident Evil* is the game that blew it up to be a success. Developed by

Capcom and first released in 1996, this is the franchise most associated with the horror game genre and had a huge impact on evolving game design. I could easily write a design book solely on the *Resident Evil* series, and I will be referencing it heavily in future chapters of this book. *Resident Evil* was in development for many years and went through redesigns as it switched consoles and new technology was released. The game was originally conceived as a remake to *Sweet Home* in one of the earlier designs, which was completely scrapped by the time the game was released. The game's lead designer was Shinji Mikami, who would have an enormous impact on the franchise and horror that I will discuss with later game examples and designs.

The story followed a special forces team known as S.T.A.R.S. in the fictional city of Racoon City. When a string of weird murders began to show up in the wilderness, the team went to investigate and found themselves trapped in a mansion full of zombies. Even though the use of zombies in videogame and media became an overused trope, *Resident Evil* was the first game to use the now iconic monster this way and started the trend (Figure 3.4).

Like *Alone in the Dark*, players could choose from two different characters, Chris Redfield and Jill Valentine, but *Resident Evil* featured unique storylines depending on who the player picked. Jill's run was arguably the easier of the two: having access to stronger weapons and an easier path through. Everything about *Resident Evil* was a more refined version of the design seen in *Alone in the Dark*.

The mansion was rendered in 3D while still making use of fixed camera angles. Where *Alone in the Dark* focused on close-ranged combat and clunky guns, *Resident Evil* was the opposite. The different firearms were your main way of fighting enemies and the player had to effectively manage their ammo reserves. A knife was available as a last resort and was the weakest weapon in the game.

Figure 3.4

Resident Evil would go on to become the most recognizable horror franchise with its design copied and iterated on for years to come.

Puzzles were spread throughout the mansion requiring the player to explore for the items and clues needed to complete them. Solving a puzzle would either unlock the way towards a new area or provide the player with the potential solution to another puzzle. The larger game space also expanded into a separate greenhouse area and an underground lab. Unlike *Alone in the Dark*, the puzzles and general exploration focused more on action gameplay. There were different enemy types, but all enemies could be killed. There were far less death traps, and the puzzle logic was more straightforward.

Besides the obvious horror tones of fighting zombies and monsters in the dark, *Resident Evil* would set many staples of survival horror gameplay that I will discuss in the next chapter. Inventory management was key as stronger weapons had less ammo compared to the regular handgun. In the back half of the game, the most dangerous non-boss enemy, hunters, would populate the mansion and would require stronger weapons to deal with them easily. By this point in the game industry, hardware technology was at the point where it was possible to create and render scary enemies. *Resident Evil* would also be credited for several iconic and infamous moments in horror. The zombie reveal cutscene gave players chills, and the Cerberus enemy breaking through the window was one of the first ever uses of the "**jump scare**" in a horror game.

Despite the horror, the game also made use of B-movie cheesy writing to lighten the mood. Besides the opening **FMV** intro to the characters, two lines that fans quote to this day are about Jill having to avoid becoming a "Jill sandwich" and her being "the master of unlocking."

Resident Evil as a franchise would become the standard of horror design multiple times over the years, and it cannot be understated the impact it has had on the game industry (Figure 3.5). I will be returning to it many times throughout this book to discuss relevant elements that showed up in later entries. In terms of success,

Figure 3.5

The remake of *Resident Evil* 1 is considered one of the best by adding in new content and challenges and vastly improving the graphics.

3. The Rise of Survival Horror

the series has had its ups and downs just as the horror genre that I will discuss in Chapter 7. At the time of writing this, there are nine main entries (including the prequel *Resident Evil Zero*), remakes of the original trilogy, multiple spinoffs (some in completely different genres), a movie franchise, a Netflix show, and a new game: *Resident Evil Village*.

3.4 Silent Hill

The last franchise I will be dedicating an entire section to in this chapter is like the other side of the coin compared to *Resident Evil*. *Silent Hill* was developed by Konami under the "Team Silent" development group, and the first game was released in 1999. The story followed Harry Mason who was traveling to the town of *Silent Hill* with his adopted daughter Cheryl. Upon arriving, they had a mysterious car crash and Cheryl disappeared, requiring Harry to go search for her in the abandoned town.

Immediately, *Silent Hill* stood out from *Resident Evil* by being able to manipulate the 3D camera instead of just fixed angles (Figure 3.6). Unlike the heroes of *Resident Evil*, Harry was just a regular man with no combat training. This was displayed in game with how he frantically handled melee weapons and the small assortment of guns. The series also introduced the infamous radio that would show up in later entries and acted as a warning to the player when enemies were nearby but have not been seen yet. The radio, despite giving an early warning, was a great source of tension thanks to informing the player that something is about to attack, but not giving any indication where or what it is.

Silent Hill stood out from the other horror games thanks to a focus on the location itself. The town of *Silent Hill* is just as iconic as the story and characters

Figure 3.6

Having a 3D camera afforded the developers of *Silent Hill* the chance of showing the game from unusual angles to further heighten the weird scenes.

of the series which I will come back to in a second. Instead of just taking place in one section of the town, players had to explore major landmarks like the school and hospital. The general plot of each game is that the town of *Silent Hill* morphs based on the person experiencing it, and this manifests itself with "other" versions of the town that are far more disturbing. Even though the games never featured multiple protagonists, each title had multiple endings.

Where *Resident Evil* has a focus on combat over adventure gameplay, *Silent Hill* was the reverse. Each major location in the game was its own self-contained level with puzzles to solve and enemies to fight. The items and solutions to a puzzle were always found in the same location and made it easier to figure them out compared to adventure games. This kind of progression also created an interesting **dynamic** between the horror and the gameplay. Most horror games keep the player constantly in tense situations (and something I will talk more about in the next chapter). By switching between the normal and other version of the town, it provided the player with moments of respite to help calm them down before raising the tension again with another transition. While there were plenty of enemies and bosses, combat was not supposed to be what the player focused on.

Finally, what made *Silent Hill* as a franchise unique to this day was this idea of a mature horror game. There is a reason why I said that *Silent Hill* and *Resident Evil* were like two sides of the same coin. *Resident Evil* represents the over-the-top B-movie side – where villains give cheesy monologues and places self-destruct at the end. *Silent Hill* represents something more primal and sinister and took videogames into psychological horror. There is never a point in any *Silent Hill* where the game stops and explains to the player what is going on. Each game has a two-fold mystery to it – what is happening to the protagonist and what can the player learn about *Silent Hill*? The ending of a *Resident Evil* title is a moment of joy and victory for their protagonist over the situation; the ending of a *Silent Hill* title is more about comprehending the sights and horrors that were witnessed.

For the first time in a horror series, *Silent Hill* presented **lore** or backstory beyond just the main character. There were rules to how the world worked and the creatures the player had to go up against. This focus on lore would be copied and refined by many indie games in the 2010s, and I will discuss this concept more in Section 5.4. The mystery aspect was further heightened thanks to the disturbing enemy and environmental designs that the series became famous for. While *Resident Evil* gave us some iconic moments, *Silent Hill* would give us one of the most iconic monsters in all of videogame horror: *Silent Hill 2*'s "Pyramid Head" (Figure 3.7). The creature was a manifestation of protagonist James Sunderland's need for punishment and frustration about his wife's death. The second game featured enemy designs of mannequin like creatures with an amalgamation of limbs.

Silent Hill would go on to have a total of seven main entries and several spinoffs done by other developers. Fans consider the original trilogy to be the best, with many pointing to a decline in quality in the later games that were not worked

Figure 3.7

Pyramid Head's introduction was famous for how off-putting and disturbing it was, and became one of the most iconic videogame characters because of it despite never speaking.

on by Team Silent. There were plans for a reboot known as *Silent Hills* helmed by the famous designer of the *Metal Gear Solid* series Hideo Kojima, but a falling out between him and Konami cancelled that project. At the time of writing this book, there have been rumors that the project may be back on, but nothing concrete at this time.

Silent Hill and *Resident Evil* represent the two popular forms of horror that other developers have been modeling their games after for years and were the kings of the survival horror genre.

3.5 A Snapshot of Scares

Whenever I have history chapters in the *Game Design Deep Dive* series, I feel it is important to provide the reader with a snapshot at other notable games to show the impact of the genre. Survival horror at its height lasted nine years – from 1996 to 2005, with several smaller titles released beforehand. In that span of time, I saw a variety of horror games that tried to position themselves as the king of survival horror.

The *Clock Tower* series developed by Human Entertainment was ahead of Capcom by being released in 1995 for the Super Famicom (or SNES in the US) (Figure 3.8). Just like *Sweet Home*, the game remained exclusive to Japan, but later entries were ported globally. The first two games were played as a point and click-styled adventure, with the third adopting a survival horror style. The series involved people being stalked by the serial killer "Scissorman." This would also be the first horror game to have enemies actively chasing the player which I will discuss more in the next chapter.

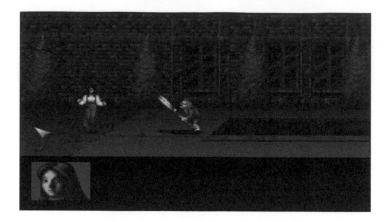

Figure 3.8

Many survival horror games during this period featured normal people (often women and girls) having to stay alive and fight against the monsters after them.

D developed by the late Kenji Edo and Warp was an interactive movie that used FMV during the peak of that style in 1995. The game became famous for the period thanks to its disturbing scenes and strict two-hour play limit. It would go on to have two sequels *Enemy Zero* and *D2*. As with the *Clock Tower* series, the gameplay does not hold up as well compared to *Resident Evil* and *Silent Hill*.

Another FMV-styled horror game was *Phantasmagoria* also released in 1995 designed by Roberta Williams and Sierra (Figure 3.9). The game made use digitized actors and computer and practical effects to tell its story, which sparked controversy for featuring very explicit acts of violence including sexual assault. This style of very graphic adventure games would be used by other developers during the 1990s which could be argued was a way of giving a game free publicity and shock value.

Capcom tried to strike gold twice with the *Dino Crisis* series first released in 1999 and was created by Shinji Mikami. Instead of zombies and monsters, the series had players fighting against dinosaurs who have been genetically cloned and let loose in different locales. There was far more action to the series compared to *Resident Evil*. With only three main entries in the series, it has become a kind of cult classic for fans who have been waiting for a reboot.

Another cult classic franchise was *Fatal Frame* by Tecmo (now known as Koei Tecmo) with the original release in Japan in 2001. The series focused on fighting Japanese ghosts using a magical camera known as the "Camera Obscura," which was the only way to defend yourself. *Fatal Frame* was closer to *Silent Hill* in terms of pacing and its core gameplay loop. There were far less enemies to fight, but each one was a challenge of trying to use the camera obscura to get the best shot, also known as a "fatal frame." Enemy designs were ghosts of people with their limbs and bodies twisted and contorted. The controlling of the tension was a major point

Figure 3.9

The PC was home to many horror adventure games that pushed the envelope during the 1990s.

of fear that I will be discussing more in Section 5.2. At this moment, there are five games in the series, one that was exclusive to Japan, and a Nintendo 3DS spinoff. Unfortunately, low sales of the later games have ended the series for now. As a quick tangent, *Fatal Frame 3: The Tormented* released in 2005 is the game I credit as the one that managed to scare the terror of playing horror games out of me.

The final series I want to mention in this chapter is *Siren* developed by Project Siren which was a development team in the studio "Japan Studio" first released in 2003. Just like *Fatal Frame, Siren* focused heavily on Japanese horror. The story was told from ten different characters trying to survive after their town was stricken with a curse and most of the people turned into monsters known as Shibitos. Unlike the other horror games mentioned, *Siren* is one of the hardest survival horror games ever made going into it for the first time. Not only did players have to avoid the enemies using stealth, as it was impossible to kill them, but the story could only be moved along by performing specific tasks with different characters. It was possible to "sight jack" enemies, allowing them to see from the enemy's viewpoint. Many critics called out the difficulty of the game which was corrected in later entries. Currently, there are three entries and no plans to continue it.

There were many other survival horror games released during this period, but this should give you a good idea of the variety of the genre.

4

Basic Horror Design

Figure 4.1

Horror is more about creating an atmosphere and theme rather than individual mechanics or gameplay loops.

DOI: 10.1201/9781003199250-4

4.1 Defining the Horror Genre

Before I begin examining design elements, there is something important I need to discuss and why writing a book on the design of horror is so difficult. "Horror" in and of itself is not a mechanical descriptor of game design in the same way as "platformer," "roguelike," or any other game genre I will discuss in the *Game Design Deep Dive* series. Horror is more about a philosophy or theme that can be applied to *any* gameplay genre, and the indie scene is proof positive of this and will be discussed in Chapter 8 (Figure 4.1).

What that means for the purpose of this book is that it is impossible to provide you with a "standard design," unless I literally explain the mechanics of every genre that exists in the industry. Instead, our design chapters will focus on mechanics and **systems** that have been made popular by horror designers in the past, and the philosophies of horror design. The philosophical nature is important to learn, as that is what makes a story or product horror regardless of the medium.

To define horror for this book, it will be producing a videogame (or any work) with the goal to scare the consumer or make them unease. There are examples of non-horror games that could still scare someone by using the elements throughout this book, whether intentionally or not that I will come back to in Chapter 9. It is entirely possible to the philosophy and methods discussed in this book in non-horror games as a way of heightening the mood and creating tension.

Horror at the end of the day will remain forever niche due to the very fact that a lot of people do not like being terrified by the products they use. This is important to consider when deciding to make a horror game and what market you will find; a topic I will discuss more in Chapter 10.

One last point before I begin, horror at its best is not about bombastic scenes and explosions, but subtle elements that can create and elevate the tension. You do not need expensive game engines and the best art team to make a scary game, but simply understanding the philosophy behind horror that I will go into detail about in the next chapter.

4.2 What Is Survival Horror

The last chapter was a brief history lesson of the horror genre up until 2005 and was populated by "survival horror." Another challenge of discussing horror from a design standpoint is that the genre has taken radically different paths in terms of philosophy in the past 16 years from indie to **AAA** studios. For the first design lesson on horror, I want to talk specifically about the gameplay loop of survival horror, because this is the most basic form of the design for developers to start out with (Figure 4.2).

Returning to Section 3.2, survival horror was first defined by *Alone in the Dark* as the combination of adventure and action-styled gameplay. If you want your game to be considered survival horror, then both kinds of design must be

Figure 4.2

Survival Horror is about having both adventure and action-focused gameplay at the same time, and removing one would change the game into a different form of horror.

present – solving puzzles and looking for clues for adventure, fighting enemies and staying alive for action.

A key difference between traditional action games and survival horror is that there is a focus on resource management – health, ammunition, etc. The balance of resources is an important aspect that will be discussed in Chapter 6. For now, a big part of the philosophy or horror, and what separates horror from other genres, is how at ease is the player at any given moment. Action games are about putting the player into a position of power – letting them cut loose with all manner of weapons and destruction. Resources in an action game are often abundant or easy to refill. One of the major design changes of action games in the modern market has been giving the player the ability to refill or regenerate essential resources to keep them in the action.

The *survival* part of survival horror is about keeping the player in a state of unease in terms of their resources. As the designer, you want the player to be asking themselves the following questions: "Do I have enough ammo to fight?" "Is it worth it to use my gun now? "Should I risk fighting this thing?" This becomes increasingly hard to do the longer a game gets and gets at the challenge of effective pacing that I will discuss in Chapter 9.

Any videogame where the player can be hurt will also have health management besides ammo. The act of healing is often made a necessity, as some horror games will slow the character down when they are near death or after taking a certain amount of damage. As I will discuss throughout this book, later examples of horror games have taken different liberties when it comes to a health/healing system, with many modern ones simply having the enemy kill the player instantly if they are caught.

You want the player to be exploring for more resources and items to solve the various puzzles. To help the player out, many horror titles will provide a map function as part of the **UI**. The map allows the player to see where they have been and what areas are left to explore. Later examples further enhanced the map by indicating if a room still had items in it to be discovered. It is important when placing ammo reserves in the world to always give more than what is needed, as players can end up wasting ammo with missed shots or being startled. This is also why the *Resident Evil* series always gives the player a knife or melee option, to prevent them from becoming stuck and not able to get past enemies or known as a **soft lock** situation.

There is a careful balance of introducing more elements that give the player power and those that take it away. A common pacing problem is not introducing new threats and situations to keep the player on their toes. In Section 9.4, I will elaborate on pacing issues and how to try and get around them.

Survival horror may provide the basic framework for horror, but it is quite easy to mess up that foundation. Putting too much of a focus on the action gameplay will result in the player being more concerned about that instead of being scared. However, removing combat results in the game becoming repetitive, and I will go more into detail about this balance in Chapter 6.

4.3 Controls and Camera Design

Coming up with a functional UI is an essential part of any game design, and chapters detailing this will be featured in every *Game Design Deep Dive* book. Determining what camera system to use is entirely up to the developer, and there have been horror game examples using a wide variety. Because I am focusing on survival horror now, I will stick with the popular examples.

Figure 4.3

Resident Evil popularized both the fixed camera system and tank-like controls which retained its popularity until the rise of action horror design.

The first major type was a fixed camera system, which simply means that the player has no control over how the game shows what is happening (Figure 4.3). Originally, this was used to get around the technical constraints of early consoles and PCs, but it does present some unique advantages and disadvantages for horror design. By controlling the angles and viewpoint of the player, the designer knows exactly where the player is looking and focusing when determining how to scare them. This led to fixed angle cameras having a more cinematic feel to them. A popular example of a jump scare is to simply place an enemy behind a corner or off camera when the player is moving around an area. When the player makes that turn or moves to the next screen, the enemy will be waiting to attack them. I will discuss more about jump scares in Section 4.5.

The problem with this setup is that many modern gamers find this style to be dated when paired with the control system used in *Resident Evil* that I will discuss in a minute. This kind of camera system could become very disorienting depending on the number of angles used for a room. Smaller rooms would normally have two or three different angles, with some specifically meant to show off an important item. Larger areas could have several more, and it was easy to lose track of where you were going if each angle completely shifted the scene. Figuring out the orientation of a room proved to be difficult when only viewed from different angles and made the in-game map an important UI element.

A 3D or dynamic camera system shows everything around the player and could be controlled. The popular option is to tie camera controls either to the right analog stick for gamepads or using the mouse for computer games. When full 3D became the norm of the game industry in the late 1990s, camera relative movement became the standard control system that I will come back to later this section. While they were more complicated to design, they offered an easier way for players to experience the game (Figure 4.4).

Figure 4.4

A 3D camera allows the player to control it and see far more around them than a fixed one and has become a standard for most action-based designs.

There is a lot about 3D camera system design that is beyond the scope of this book. For horror game's specifically, they would often use either the over-the-shoulder system (that became the standard of action-horror design) or a slightly overhead system. Besides the added complexity, 3D camera systems could prove frustrating depending on their design and the environment. If the player backed up into a wall or was in a tight corridor, it was easy for the camera to get stuck and not show the player what was happening. It was also harder to surprise the player with enemies appearing off screen when they could simply change the angle and spot an oncoming threat.

The camera system would have an impact on the controls that developers would use for horror. In the previous chapter, I talked about the differences between *Resident Evil* (specifically the original trilogy) and *Silent Hill* in terms of controls. *Resident Evil*'s style of having the controls based on the character and not the camera led to the style of tank-like controls. This meant that the player could not just immediately move in a different direction but had to manually turn the character first before moving.

Due to movement being based on the angle the camera was viewing them, this often led to the controls getting in the way when trying to do something and made movement far more complicated than in other genres. The player could not just immediately run away from an enemy that was coming at them; they had to turn their character one position at a time before they could start moving.

An advantage of this system was that because movement was not tied to the camera itself, it was a little easier to control a character when the camera angle shifted. One important UI detail that developers did was to lock movement independently of the camera while a character was moving. What that meant was once a character starts moving in one direction, they will keep moving in said direction no matter how the camera angle or orientation shifts. Once the player stops moving their character, the movement will become affected by the camera. While this was used with the tank-like system, it was far more important for a camera relative movement system.

Camera relative movement is the design of moving a character relative to the camera (Figure 4.5). With a tank-like system, pressing "left" would simply start turning the character left. With a relative system, pressing "left" would cause the character to start moving to the left side of the screen. This control system was more natural compared to tank-like controls, and why it became the standard for 3D games.

Besides the added complexity to design, camera relative systems needed to be fine-tuned to avoid issues. Above, I mentioned how a 3D camera could get stuck on the environment and made it hard for the player to see. With movement tied to the camera, this could lead to frustration of the player not being able to easily get the camera unstuck so they could start moving properly again.

A common issue with 3D cameras and camera relative movement was when the camera had to switch angles based on the environment. If the player wanted to go north and they were pressing "up," up could easily become going west if the camera shifted to a different viewing angle, such as changing the angle to better

Figure 4.5

Camera relative movement ties how the character moves to how the camera is showing the action and provides far more reliable and intuitive control over a character.

show an upcoming series of obstacles. Therefore, locking movement independently from the camera became an important feature to design with movement systems.

During the early 2000s, when technology was improving on the consoles, there was a kind of hybrid model between having a fixed and dynamic camera. Games like *Resident Evil Code Veronica* (first released in 2000, and later remastered for other platforms) had the camera worked at fixed angles and directions but would pan and follow the player up until a point when it would switch to a new angle.

In terms of which system pairing is better, classic survival horror fans still like the more cinematic feel of fixed camera angles, but 3D cameras offer more utility and functionality for the player. Depending on who you talk to, some like tank-like controls as a way of limiting the player's ability to control their character and add tension, while others like the greater control of camera relative movement. In my opinion, if you are thinking about designing a horror game aimed at the modern market, you want to go with 3D and camera relative movement. However, there are indie developers that I will discuss in Chapter 8 who purposely ignore that for the classic feel.

While I will be talking about over the shoulder system in Chapter 7 for action-horror, first-person horror has become exceedingly popular. It allows for the best of both worlds: giving the player full control over their character but limiting their viewpoint to whatever the camera is pointing at and allowing for some scary moments. Many of the most popular indie horror games that will come up in Chapter 8 were made using a first-person perspective. The reason why I am not spending a lot of time on it is that there really is not much to say that is done differently with the system compared to first-person shooters. The one aspect that is different is how event triggers work that I will discuss more in Section 4.5.

4.4 World Design

The philosophy of horror and world design often go together as one affects the other. Horror works best in terms of creating tension when there is a localized or smaller-scale environment and something I will come back to in Chapter 5. Horror games in general avoid the standard stage-based approach that consumers see from action titles and go with their own take on nonlinear gameplay (Figure 4.6).

The player is often free to explore multiple parts of the environment looking for resources and items to move things along. To make progress, there will always be a specific item or event that must be done to unlock the next area, but the player is free to spend however long they want while exploring. The player can return to previous areas to find additional resources, and many survival horror games require them to return to visit previously inaccessible areas.

The *Silent Hill* series had one of the best takes on world design by focusing on the town itself. Players would explore the neighborhoods and various streets to find resources and get to the next major area. As I discussed in the previous chapter, the structure of *Silent Hill* had each major area being its own encapsulated stage. To move the story along and get to the next place, the player had to finish all the puzzles and often fight one final boss monster for that area.

Figure 4.6

The world design of a horror game will dictate the flow of the game and how to measure someone's progress through it.

4. Basic Horror Design

The technology at the time of development had a factor on world design. Due to the limited hardware power of early consoles, the first horror games could only load and render so much that could be displayed at once. *Resident Evil* turned this into a style by showing a first-person cutscene of a door opening when transitioning from one room to the next. One of the most famous examples of developer ingenuity was the now infamous fog used in *Silent Hill*. The game was purposely foggy in the outdoor sections as the game engine could not properly render areas far away from the player without slowing the game down. This ended up working incredibly well with the aesthetic and added to the tension of not being able to see what was coming down the street. In fact, when the first game was remade and re-released in 2012 without the fog, fans found that it made the game aesthetically worse for them.

Another style that I have seen become popular with indie developers is a **hub**-focused world. Hub areas are typically associated with games where the player must return to a home base or centralized area between stages. For horror games, developers will often let the player return to the hub after each major area. They can use this time to unwind, study any notes or items found, and begin looking for the next area to continue the story. Depending on the game's design, some will allow the player to revisit a previously completed area, and others will prevent it. A similar example is a chapter format, where each chapter takes place in a different area and is self-contained, once the player finishes a chapter they cannot return to that same area unless a later chapter revisits it (Figure 4.7).

These styles are the basic and most often used examples of world design in horror. There are exceptions and more advanced takes on world design that I will return to in Chapter 9. The world of your game is going to impact all aspects of

Figure 4.7

A hub and chapter format makes it easier to compartmentalize each area into a unique situation; keeping the player guessing as to what is coming next.

the design and balance of the game mechanics. In Chapter 6, I will discuss more about what the player is going to be doing in the world and how to fill it with obstacles.

4.5 Event Triggers

For the final section of this chapter, it is important to discuss the concept of **event triggers** (or trigger events) and how they relate to not just horror but all game design. An event trigger is simply a conditional situation that causes the game to do something. Event triggers have been used since the very beginning of the game industry as ways of telling the game how to update the player's score or know when the player has won or lost.

Many cinematic games will use event triggers to guide the player through a high-stakes scene – setting off explosions or destroying paths when the player reaches a specific point to push them in the right direction (Figure 4.8). The style of setting up areas that everything is predetermined is often referred to as a "scripted event." The purpose of event triggers is to direct the game to react a specific way at certain points, and why they are critical for horror design.

In the next chapter, I will be discussing the philosophy behind horror and part of that is being able to manipulate and control the situation around the player to keep the tension exactly right. Horror games have been effectively (and not so effectively) using event triggers to keep players on their toes since *Alone in the Dark*. A basic example is to cause a monster attack when the player reaches a specific point or picks up an important item. Many action games will set up traps like this called "monster closets" that will reveal enemies all around the player once they do something. In Chapter 3, I discussed how *Resident Evil* 1 is credited

Figure 4.8

Scripted events are often used for cinematic or blockbuster moments but will often reduce the player's impact on the situation.

by having the first use of a jump scare and jump scare event triggers are the most popular example in horror games today that I will go into more detail about in Section 5.3.

Advanced examples that have been used will trigger based on where the player is looking to try and scare them with something appearing suddenly. To do this, developers will use sights and sounds to direct the player to look at a specific area, when the camera and/or character position are there, the game will generate the predefined jump scare. Astute players can get around this by purposely not looking in the intended area and trigger the jump scare knowing where it is going to show up.

In terms of gameplay, event triggers have been used heavily in survival horror design as a way of setting up additional challenges or forcing the player to adapt to a new situation. The problem from a design standpoint is that event triggers are purely conditional, which means once the player knows what event sets them off, it becomes easy to mitigate any impact they have on the game. In the *Resident Evil 2* remake released by Capcom in 2019, the game's principal enemy, Mr. X, would actively track and chase the player around. This would be an example of having an **alpha antagonist** that will be looked at more in Chapter 9. Mr. X was programmed to appear once the player reached a specific point during the game. Once someone knew where that was, it was easy to perform all the other tasks first and minimize his impact on the game (Figure 4.9).

A better use of event triggers for gameplay would be to have different conditionals for the event to keep the player guessing or even having different responses that could be chosen when the trigger goes off. Ultimately, the goal of a successful horror game is to keep the player engaged and uncertain about what is to come from beginning to end.

Figure 4.9

Mr. X appearing at this moment in the *Resident Evil 2* remake is an event trigger, because it occurs the same way every time based on the player's actions.

5

The Philosophy behind Horror

Figure 5.1

The basic element of fear in horror movies is about being stalked by some unknown entity with no idea when they're going to strike next.

DOI: 10.1201/9781003199250-5

31

5.1 The Psychology of Fear

At the start of this book, I talked about why horror is different from other game genres. Horror is not about a specific mechanic or game system, but an overall philosophy or theme that must be present (Figure 5.1). Horror at the end of the day is about fear, and more specifically, making the consumer afraid or unnerved while playing.

At the heart of this philosophy is the basic fear of the unknown. To quote H.P. Lovecraft, "The oldest and strongest emotion of mankind is fear, and the oldest and strongest kind of fear is fear of the unknown." Horror is about putting the audience into a situation where they do not know what is going to happen. Once the audience is in on the trick in a manner of speaking, they will no longer be terrified by the situation and something I will return to in Section 5.2.

Keeping the player in the dark for as long as possible is important for maintaining fear and is often the problem with long-running horror franchises. From film to TV to videogames, the longer a franchise goes on for, the harder it becomes to keep someone surprised. This often leads to creators either overexplaining to try and make sense of it all or continuing to escalate to the point where the whole situation does not make sense. This kind of challenge has led to indie developers focusing on small takes on horror that will be examined in Chapter 8 (Figure 5.2).

Putting the audience into the right mood for horror requires getting their undivided attention. Many of the most successful takes on horror keep everything that is not scary downplayed or muted. Music is often kept on the quiet side or fades in the background unless something is about to happen. When the music does pick up, that is an indication to the audience that it is time for something bad, such as the famous theme from the movie *Jaws*.

Figure 5.2

Smaller scale horror often ends after the big reveal or is short enough that the player remains tense the entire time through it.

Everything that I have talked about and will discuss in this book about the design of horror is about keeping the fear of the unknown present, as once it is gone, it will not come back. Part of the challenge behind designing a good horror game is walking that line between hiding enough of how things work to keep the player guessing, but not revealing so much that they can see the smoke and mirrors. There have been many smaller and indie horror games released in the 2010s that were too limited in terms of their mechanics that the only way to win was playing the game as mechanically as possible. That meant knowing beforehand how enemies reacted, the correct path through, and completely removed any sense of horror. There is more to discuss about keeping the player scared that I will talk about in Chapters 6 and 9.

5.2 Creating and Releasing Tension

Horror philosophy is about creating tension, or a sense of unease, with the audience or consumer. The difference between effective and not so effective horror is how tension is built up and released during play. The act of feeling tense is not exclusive to horror games, but any title where there are stakes in what is happening and a punishment for failure. Two effective examples of non-horror would be **soulslikes** and roguelikes and how dying comes with a huge cost. For soulslikes, the player is put into a position where death brings back all the defeated enemies, and a second death could cost them all the experience/money they have collected. For roguelikes, death ends the run and puts the player back to the beginning again.

Building up tension in horror is about creating an atmosphere that the player knows something is going to happen, but they have no idea where or when. This can be achieved in many ways – from turning out lights, the sudden playing of

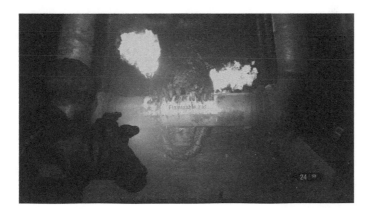

Figure 5.3

Tension releasing can be a moment of horror or a moment of triumph after a stressful situation.

music, just the very fact that they have not been attacked in a few minutes, and much more. In the previous chapter, I talked about event triggers, and having the player know that they are about to unleash something bad, but not know what said thing is, can be an effective way of raising tension. Tension can be built up for minutes at a time, but there must always come a point when it must be released. This can be positively by clearing a section or getting to a safe point, or negatively in the form of something scaring (or trying to scare) the player (Figure 5.3).

The negative release of tension is often the main reason why someone may not be a fan of horror, as not everyone likes to jump out of their seat when trying to enjoy something. While jump scares are a popular example of releasing tension, there are other ways such as being introduced to a new enemy, watching a cutscene, finishing the section, or getting a reward or upgrade.

With both the acts of raising and releasing the tension, there are difficulties with each. Tension can only be raised by keeping the player in the dark about what is happening. In the last section, I spoke about how once someone loses the fear of the unknown, they will not be scared by the game again. If the game just keeps raising the tension and not releasing it, the player will start to calm down on their own and realize that the game is not going to scare them. This is often the problem seen in horror games by first-time developers who will create a scary situation, but never do anything to release the tension.

With releasing the tension, each method can only truly work once in each game, as the player will expect the same or similar methods used after that point. This is often the problem with jump scares that I will return to in Section 5.3. As the designer, you do not want to keep releasing tension, as each time will have diminishing results.

The buildup and release of tension is a crucial part of horror in any medium, as without it, no one is going to feel scared (Figure 5.4). It is possible to frame

Figure 5.4

The problem that action horror faced was that due to the ever-escalating stakes and scenes, it was more about an adrenaline rush rather than creating tension.

the structure of your content around the buildup and release of tension to better calm the audience down, and then ratchet things back up. In Chapter 3, I spoke about *Silent Hill* and *Fatal Frame* and both series integrated their progression into the acts of raising and lowering tension. *Silent Hill*'s use of having two versions of the town allowed the player to relax (or release tension) a little when they are back in the normal version and then raised it back up when the town transformed. In both *Fatal Frame 3* and *Silent Hill 4* (released in 2004), their stories were based on leaving and going somewhere scary, and then returning to a safe area to learn more about the plot. Both games would eventually have scares in the safe parts that would catch players completely unaware.

Even horror books when framed right can raise and release tension as demonstrated by the works of famed manga artist Junji Ito. In many of his stories, characters would react to something disturbing that the reader will not see until they turn the page. This raised the tension and let them know that there was going to be some disturbing sight that often filled the entire page waiting for them.

As a designer, you will need to think as much about the buildup and release of tension as you will the general path and progression of your game. If the design of your game is not working, or the player gets stuck or annoyed, then all the work that was put into the atmosphere and tension will be lost. The next chapter will focus on the gameplay and elements that will go together with the tension.

5.3 The Use of Jump Scares

Jump scares are one of the most popular options in all parts of horror as a way of releasing tension, but their use requires more care than you would think. Over the last decade with the rise of indie horror, there have been many titles released that rely on nothing but jump scares as the only horror aspect (Figure 5.5).

Figure 5.5

Jump scares have proven to be an effective way of releasing tension but are harder to use right than one might think.

Good jump scares must relate to the situation and environment at hand. There are some games that would just play a scary note and had no relation to the area the player was in. The problem with over relying on jump scares is that it is viewed as a "cheap" way of trying to make a horror game. The more jump scares are used, the more the player becomes resistant to their impact. In Section 4.5, I talked about how jump scares are programmed around event triggers. Due to the triggers themselves being fixed events, it means that jump scares quickly lose their effectiveness once the player knows what to expect.

Raising the tension requires putting the player into a state of unease and dread, and that comes with keeping them in the dark about what is going to happen. Too many titles telegraph their jump scares to the point that it is less about being scared and more about the annoyance that it is coming up. An example would be suddenly making the music get louder or losing control of their character for a scripted event. The reason why jump scares worked so well in the first horror games was that no one knew to expect them, and they were used sparingly. There are also cases of programming them to be randomized, such as having random noises after a specific time has passed.

Another detail is in the use of the jump scare itself. Some of the best jump scares in games were understated, such as walking out of a room and seeing an enemy standing there that just appeared or something appearing in the distance where there was not anything a second ago. Many horror games rely on making the jump scare so obnoxious that it becomes annoying, such as relying on a deafening noise that can be painful for headphone users.

A final point about jump scares is what happens after and where a lot of developers fail to maintain their horror. Too many horror games only focus on the jump scare itself but not do anything while the player is shocked. In the original *Resident Evil*, when the Cerberus jumped through the window for the first time, that was not a cutscene, *that was an actual attack that the player had to respond to* (Figure 5.6).

Horror designers today will often do one of two things with their jump scares. The jump scare is just the signal that the player has died and there is nothing else that comes after it other than restarting the game. The other option is that the jump scare is used to simply break up the monotony of exploring, but then the player gets right back to exploring after the shock has worn off. The best uses of jump scares lead to something – forcing the shocked player to now react to the stressful situation. In the *Resident Evil 2* remake and the *Resident Evil 3* remake (released in 2020), the arrival of Mr.X and Nemesis, respectively, was always done as a jump scare, and then, the player needed to think quickly to get away from them.

5.4 Telling Scary Stories

Writing the story to anything horror-related is important, as part of what connects us is the human element. Some of the most effective horror stories regardless of the

Figure 5.6

The best jump scares force the player to react to what follows, and why the original *Resident Evil* 1 scare seen here was one of the most memorable.

medium are built on low stakes. It is not about the world ending, but the impact on a few lives (Figure 5.7). Part of the problem with long running franchises has been this need to raise the stakes with each new one. *Friday the 13th* started with a killer in a hocky mask terrorizing a camp; later entries had Jason returning from hell or being a nanomachine-infused super killer in the far future.

In Chapter 7, I will talk about how *Resident Evil* as a franchise collapsed under the weight of it overdesign, and part of that was making the story more and more outlandish. By *Resident Evil 6*, the story spanned the entire globe, and the stakes were the end of humanity.

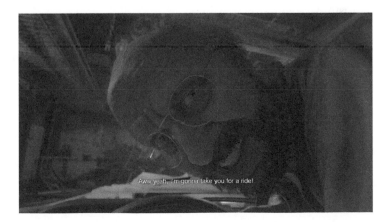

Figure 5.7

A good horror story is as much about the protagonist dealing with what's going on as it is the monsters coming after them.

Part of the appeal of psychological horror is the human element and watching someone go through, and hopefully survive, a traumatic situation. Audiences resonated with the characters of the *Silent Hill* series because they were average people put into unusual situations with no special powers or military training to help them. Returning to the works of Junji Ito, his stories are all about everyday people trying to live through something horrible, with many ending darkly.

In the next chapter, I will discuss the issue of getting around the power fantasy inherent to videogames, but part of that also has to do with the story and characterizations. Having a well-written main character can go a long way towards making the audience care about them and feel terrified of losing them if they fail.

Over the 2010s, many horror game designers embraced a form of passive storytelling that was popularized by the rise of Soulslikes like *Demon's Souls* by From Software (first released in 2009). Instead of basing the story on a character, the player explored a ruined world and learned about what happened by reading about it from the items. The main character, and the characters in the world, did not really matter to the story as all the major events had already happened.

This kind of narrative began a breakdown between lore vs. plot when it came to videogame storytelling. Lore represents the story or history of the setting itself, while plot is the story of the character or people living it. Lore, when done right, can be very enriching to a game and can be extended and expanded upon across multiple entries. Some of the most popular examples of indie horror that I will go over in Chapter 8 focused on lore to drive fan interest.

The problem with a focus on lore is that it robs the player of any connection to the story as they are not really involved. Throughout the soulslike games by From Software, the player's character is never referenced or has any input or thought on what is happening. This kind of character design goes back to the trope of the "Silent Protagonist" – where despite the main character being talked to or referenced by other characters, they never say anything, or has any motivation regarding the story.

With horror games specifically, the focus on lore makes it hard to resonate with the character or become interested in the story. Many modern horror games are all about dealing with situations and events that have already happened. Whether the main character survives or not means nothing, with many horror games just ending abruptly with the character dying. Many microhorror games have a death ending which can work if the story leading up to it is interesting, but their short playtimes make them more akin to watching a TV show than playing a full game.

The main character is often so divorced from the plot that they will never respond or have any thoughts about what is happening (Figure 5.8). Outside of maybe a few screams or rambling about what to do, the character of the story has no agency or care about said story. With that said, there are plenty of games that are designed around players creating their own character and being the person in the situation. However, good horror is about growing to care about these characters and being worried about whether they are going to survive. There is an exception

Wait. You look familiar to me... that face...

Figure 5.8

A protagonist detached from the events that's happening makes it harder to become invested in the world.

when it comes to microhorror games that are meant to be a limited experience and too short to grow that connection. I will discuss that more in Chapter 8.

Something I find interesting is how with exception to the recent *Resident Evil* games in the past 4 years, there have been very few character-driven horror games released, not even by indie developers. Some of this could be blamed on the increased work and budget of animating, writing, and maybe voicing, a main character. However, developers cannot have it both ways with having a named protagonist but do nothing to develop their personality and stake in the story. Without that connection, it is hard for the audience to become invested in what is happening.

5.5 Gruesome Graphics

As hardware and technology evolved, so did the ability to reach higher levels of graphical fidelity, and horror game designers have been making use of that with each new upgrade (Figure 5.9). One of many debated topics when it comes to horror is how gruesome or disturbing do you make the visuals? Just as there are consumers not interested in being scared, there are limits to how much gore and disturbing content someone can take in any horror property.

Violent acts and mature content have existed since the rise of horror. The entire slasher film subgenre is all about seeing how many ways there are to kill someone. Using violence is also an option to raise the tension dramatically and the first act is the most shocking. Psychological horror is not known for having too many over-the-top gruesome scenes but has certainly delved into serious topics like mental illness and sexual assault.

In the 2010s, public game engines like Unreal and Unity offered smaller developers more power and flexibility than ever before. For horror designers, this led

Figure 5.9

The graphical power of game engines today has been a boon for horror designers to get creative (and horrific) with their enemy designs and situations.

to some of the most beautiful, and beautifully disturbing, examples of horror that the industry has ever seen. There are also developers who purposely make their games retro minded that I will discuss more in Chapter 8. Shock content can certainly make a project stand out, but there is a line between making something that uses shock content to tell a story and using it in a way that seems like the property is glorifying it.

Part of the reason why indie developers have grown so far is that they are not held to any hardware or content standards that console developers and major studios faced. There have been horror games that have shown characters brutally ripped apart in high detail, and actions that I cannot say in this book. The *Outlast* series by Red Barrels first released in 2013 had players sneaking around an abandoned insane asylum and interacting with a disturbing cast of characters. In one scene, the player is captured, and the game shows the main character having his fingers chopped off. The second game released in 2017 added more gross out and disturbing content that critics said went too far in terms of graphic imagery.

With technology today, it is possible to create games with art and **aesthetics** anywhere from photorealistic, to emulating older looks, and everything in-between (Figure 5.10). From a presentation standpoint, it is important to consider how far you want to go in terms of graphical violence. Push things too far and you may end up making something too much for audiences to handle, or the content is so gratuitous and over the top that the game is no longer scary. From a market standpoint, if you intend to sell your game on major platforms that have rules for disturbing content, you may need to adjust things to get the green light. Another option indie developers have done is to release the retail version of the game as the censored version and then have optional DLC that unlocks

Figure 5.10

The right aesthetic can make something horrific without the need of powerful game engines and art.

the "unrated" version. Another point is that console holders require your game to be rated for content by an organization like the **ESRB** or **PEGI** for European markets, and the higher ratings do limit the market.

How you design the art of your game can go a long way towards its appeal as well as standing out from other games. There is no one right way of creating art and aesthetics for any videogame, let alone the horror genre. I have personally played horror games that use pixel graphics that could scare someone just as well as a game using the Unreal engine.

5.6 The One Chance of Horror

Horror is an unusual genre in that any example of it can only be truly experienced one time with fresh eyes. Playing a scary videogame for the first time is a far different experience playing it multiple times. Many fans will often go back and replay a horror game for a better ending or higher ranking, and the focus then shifts to optimization instead of experiencing the game (Figure 5.11). What that also means is that a developer only has one chance to keep the horror going from beginning to end. If at any time the player becomes frustrated, is relaxed, or even finds the game funny, then the horror portion of the experience is gone.

There are so many ways for a horror game to run out of steam or fail, and why the genre is so niche in the first place.

Just remember this: It is extremely rare for a videogame to maintain its horror over many hours. Series like *Resident Evil* often just throw any semblance of horror out the window for their final areas and replace it with a high stake set piece. If your game is only 90% horror, do not consider that as a failure. As I have discussed, the main goal as a horror designer is to keep the audience scared, or

Figure 5.11

Horror games can only be experienced one time, and often, players will reach a point where they have become accustomed to what is going on.

metaphorically in the dark, for as long as possible. Many horror games and films often go for an off-the-walls finale as one final tension release to end on.

What you want to avoid is losing the audience early on due to gameplay problems and having the story and horror go to waste. This is also why when it comes to designing a horror game, it is important to pay attention to how people are liking or disliking your gameplay. I have seen many horror titles lose their audience within the first hour and only end up with a fraction of the fanbase seeing the game through to the end. Frustrating UI elements and a poor feel to the game can also attribute to people quitting a game in frustration. A common advice given in each *Game Design Deep Dive* is that you need to have people playtesting your game and listen to their feedback when refining your gameplay. Frustrating elements are often the anthesis of good game design and get in the way of horror, and I will discuss that more in Section 9.6.

So far in this book, I have spoken about surface layer content and psychology, and it is now time to talk about the actual content and ways to make gameplay scary.

Creating Scary Gameplay

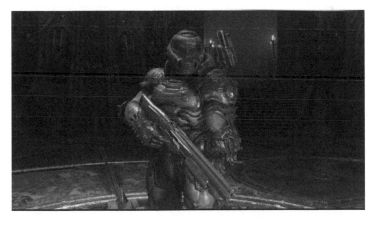

Figure 6.1

There are plenty of games that use monsters and may appear to be horror but are really about making the player feel stronger than them.

DOI: 10.1201/9781003199250-6

43

6.1 Fighting the Power Fantasy

Before I can discuss making gameplay in horror, there is an important aspect that is an always constant struggle for horror in any medium – the power fantasy. Looking at the appeal of videogames or any entertainment medium, there is an escapism element to them. The Young Adult genre is full of stories about people throwing away their normal lives and discovering they are really a powerful hero, wizard, etc.

Videogames allow us to experience situations that most of us will never achieve – winning the super bowl, saving a princess, becoming billionaires, and so many more examples. These games are about making the player feel powerful – they are the ones in charge of the situation and that are about the power fantasy of making the player feel amazing about themselves (Figure 6.1). The challenge that horror games face is trying to balance the player's own ability to control the situation with trying to keep them out of control to be scared. Looking at anything in the action genre, the hero is never scared and oftentimes makes light of their own situation. Every aspect of a videogame comes into play when determining how the player is supposed to feel while playing it. Under the right circumstances, even a game that is not in the horror genre can have moments of terror that I will come back to in Chapter 9.

As a case in point, I want to briefly describe the plot of two different videogames to show how different gameplay and aesthetics can change the mood of a game. Game #1: The player is trapped on Mars where portals to hell have opened and demons have killed everyone else with the goal of fighting back and reclaiming the planet. Game #2: The player arrives at their family home late at night to find the place is a mess, their mom, dad, and sister are missing, and their goal is to figure out what happened.

Given those two descriptions and not knowing the games I am referencing, it would be easy to assume that game #1 has more horror to it, but that is not the case. Game #1 is referencing *Doom* by ID Software and the revival that came out in 2016. *Doom* is the very definition of the power fantasy in videogames, with the main character known as "Doom Guy," a one-man demon killing machine. At no point during the game is the player ever supposed to be scared by giant demons threatening to kill them. From the first cutscene in *Doom Eternal* (released in 2020), this is the opening narration the player gets:

> Against all the evils that Hell can conjure, all the wickedness mankind can produce, we will send unto them…only you. Rip and tear, until it is done.

This was a huge difference from the opening and atmosphere of *Doom 3* released in 2004 that positioned itself far more into horror than any other entry in the series. The player had to explore darken areas slowly and were limited by health and ammo. With *Doom* 2016 and *Doom Eternal*, the developer's goal was to always make the player feel powerful and approach every fight with excitement instead of being scared. Instead of having to manage resources, the player had the means of regenerating health and ammo by killing enemies, and this was taken further in *Doom Eternal* with the "glory kill" system. At some point, there will have to be a *Game Design Deep Dive: Shooters* to go into more detail about this design.

Game #2 is *Gone Home* developed by Fullbright and released in 2013. *Gone Home* was not designed to be a horror game, but colloquially known as a "walking simulator." Exploring the home was all about putting the player into a sense of unease about where their family is. The player is never in any danger or can fail, but the atmosphere of wandering around an abandoned home worked to give the game a light horror tone. Even though the player is never handed a gun, or a monster is attacking them, the first time playing *Gone Home* can be a tense experience when the player does not know what to expect.

The differences in tone between *Doom 3* and later entries highlight the challenge of the power fantasy and how to make the player scared. Combat is about giving the player power and became a major aspect of action-horror design that I will discuss in the next chapter. The more combat in a game, the more the player becomes used to the situation and the less tense things become. In Section 9.4, I will talk more about the pacing and how that and the gameplay must be done right to keep the horror going.

The problem that many horror designers faced over the 2010s, and what led to a change in design, is that combat can ruin horror. The very first zombie attack in the original *Resident Evil* was a scary moment, but the more times the player kills a zombie, the less the impact it has. Part of the problem with maintaining horror is games that feature combat is the growing **power curve** and arsenal the player has access to. By the time an expert player reaches the final act of a *Resident Evil* game, they should have so much ammo that there is no real threat from any enemy, not even the final boss.

Figure 6.2

With the right mood and atmosphere, it is possible to create a tense situation regardless of how armed, or unarmed, the player is.

To combat this problem, many indie developers removed the ability for the player to fight any of the enemies. I will go more into examples in Chapter 8, but the first breakout example was *Amnesia the Dark Descent* by Frictional Games in 2010. Players had to regain their memories in a deserted castle while avoiding monsters and solving puzzles. The developers purposely removed any ability for the player to fight back, and their only option was to hide and avoid contact.

Removing combat has been a major part of the changes that the indie scene has made to horror (Figure 6.2). Being able to fight back gives the player some semblance of control, and not having it puts the focus on always having to react to what is going on. With that said, I have argued that completely removing the ability for the player to fight back robs a game of its horror over the long term.

Just as having too much combat puts the player in control, having nothing to fill that space with gives the player a different kind of control. Once someone knows that there is only one way to play the game to win or that there are not any actual threats coming to get them, then the feeling of fear goes away. For the player to feel terror, they need to be active in the game space. Many games feel more akin to being in a haunted house due to their overreliance on event triggers and jump scares.

When someone is scared or stressed, their body can trigger a fight or flight response. Being able to make that decision in a videogame is an important part about horror, and why many indie horror games lose their impact after a few scares. If the player knows that there is no way to fight or deal with an enemy, once they are spotted, the choice is already made for them to flee or be killed. Many games have tried to make this challenging by having the enemy be incredibly fast or attentive to noise, but that just further restricts the player's ability to have an impact on the game.

Part of the reason why survival horror was so scary was that it forced the player to ask the question, "Should I actually try to fight this thing?" How combat and the mechanics around it are designed has an impact on how terrifying it is to fight. In the game *Condemned Criminal Origins* developed by Monolith Productions and released in 2005, the player had to fight through condemned buildings battling deranged homeless people and drug addicts. Most of the combat was about fighting close-ranged and wielding whatever was nearby as a makeshift weapon. Combat was not meant to be fun or exciting, but one mini ordeal after another to survive. Conversely, *F.E.A.R.* also released by Monolith in the same year had a focus on making the player feel powerful by giving them the ability to slow down time while getting into gunfights with super soldiers. Even though there were jump scares and the game's story dealt with ghosts, they were the ones in control.

One example I always talk about when it comes to avoiding the power fantasy in horror is from the cult classic *Evil Dead 2* released in 1987 (Figure 6.3). Near the end of the movie, Ash (played by Bruce Campbell) needs to go down into a cellar where there is a monster waiting for him to recover pages of the Necronomicon. Just before this scene, the movie has the classic "hero arms

Figure 6.3

Fighting the power fantasy is not about removing the ability to fight but making it so that even if someone is armed, they do not want to think about fighting a monster.

themselves for the big fight" moment with Ash getting a double-barreled shotgun and the iconic chainsaw, before uttering his famous line "groovy." The very next scene, he is absolutely terrified in the cellar at the prospect of having to fight the monster despite being armed for the fight. Conversely, in the 2005 movie *Doom*, much of the movie is themed around horror until near the end when the main character played by Karl Urban goes on a rampage in first-person (paying homage to the videogame) with the scene scored with heavy metal.

Good horror design must strike that balance between letting the player feel like they are in control as in having an impact on what is happening, without being so in control that they are no longer terrified. To do that requires understanding what mechanics to give them and what obstacles to throw in their way.

6.2 Resource Management

Regardless of the kind of design your gameplay is built on, resource management is an essential part of horror design and what separates it from other genres. With horror being about not having the player be completely in control, having limits on resources has been an effective way of forcing the player to change their strategy. "Resources" can mean different things depending on the game in question but refer to anything that the player can use to help them that has a limit (Figure 6.4).

The two most popular kinds of resources are weapon/ammo based and recovery items. The player's ability to feel in control is dependent on how powerful they are at any given time. If someone could just use the best weapon infinitely, then there is no reason to be scared. Incidentally, many survival horror games have an infinite ammo option that is often unlocked by achieving the best possible score

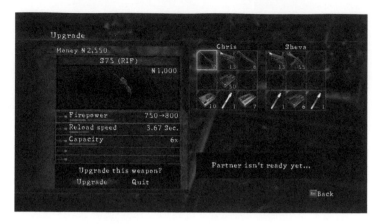

Figure 6.4

Managing inventory space is a constant challenge when the player is limited on resources.

or highest rank while playing. A simple way of categorizing weapons is by tiers, and I can use the original *Resident Evil* as an example.

- **Tier 1** – Combat Knife. Weakest weapon but can be used without any ammo and is considered the last resort.
- **Tier 2** – Handgun. Basic long-ranged weapon. Does minimal damage and requires handgun ammo which is the most common.
- **Tier 3** – Shotgun. Close ranged weapon that does moderate damage. Can be used to finish off zombies with a single headshot. Requires shotgun rounds that are harder to find.
- **Tier 4** – Grenade Launcher. Short- to mid-range weapon that does varying damage based on rounds used. Different rounds work better against different enemy types, but all grenade round types is extremely limited.
- **Tier 5** – Magnum, any range weapon. Does heavy damage and can kill any non-boss enemy in a few shots. Uses magnum ammo which is the rarest in the game.
- **Tier 6** – Rocket Launcher, any range weapon. The strongest weapon in the entire game and can kill anything in one shot. Only has one round and shows up at the very end of the game to deal with the final boss.

Some games do not use established tiers and instead have the player make the decision about what to use based on what is available. With *Condemned* mentioned last section, players had to constantly exchange weapons as they were also the tools used to get around obstacles. Every weapon had a different rating in terms of damage, speed, range, and blocking power that player had to decide what to take.

The common rule of thumb when it comes to managing and balancing ammo supplies is that the stronger the weapon, the less the ammo should be found for it. This philosophy did lead to issues where players expended their best ammo and could not deal with any boss enemies (enemy design will be discuss in the next section). One way to get around this was to always have ammo supplies and healing items in the area when fighting a boss.

Another option is to have weapon durability: When a weapon runs out of durability, it either breaks or has its stats reduced to the point of making it useless. Limiting the player's ability to fight is a great way to raise tension but can also raise frustration if weapons break too quickly for the player to replace them.

When action-horror began to grow in popularity, another element that was introduced was the concept of having randomized resources. Later entries in *Resident Evil* and other action-horror franchises would often have nondescript containers that players could break throughout the environment. What the player would find would be randomized by the game. This was a double-edged sword, as it kept the player guessing, but could lead to situations where the drops are not helping the player for the situation at hand. Later *Resident Evil* titles and the *Dead Space* series first released in 2008 by Visceral Games would tilt the system to provide ammo largely for the weapons the player was currently equipped with.

The other kinds of resources are recovery or survival items – any non-combat resource that helps the player survive. The most common example would be healing items that allow the player to recover their health after taking damage. Most horror games do not automatically recover the player's health to help add on to the tension of playing. For people who **speedrun** games, healing items can be used to purposely take damage with the intent of doing something faster. If your game has status aliments like "bleeding," "poisoned," or anything else, there should be recovery items to cure them as well.

For games that have secondary items like flashlights, many horror games will require the player to find batteries to keep their light source powered (Figure 6.5).

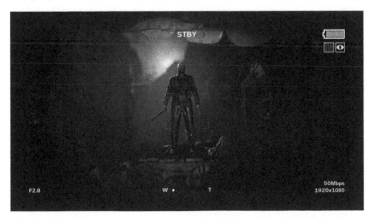

Figure 6.5

If a consumable item is required to play the game, be careful with limiting them too much, such as those that are required to see.

As a developer, you need to be careful with how required survival items are and how quickly the player can go through them. Returning to *Amnesia* the player had to keep their lantern full of oil and have recovery items to help their sanity. If the player's sanity goes too low, the screen becomes distorted and when paired with low light can cause a headache in some players.

The final part about resource management is the act of carrying them around. Inventory space in a horror game is always contested, as the player will never have enough room to carry everything they need. Part of the challenge is having to balance recovery items, weapons, ammo, and key items for solving puzzles in the player's inventory. Some horror games allow the player to find, or purchase upgraded inventory spaces, while others keep a fixed limit. Depending on the focus of the experience, you can give the player enough space to not worry about inventory as another option.

When deciding on the inventory limit, you want to look at the number of items the player is going to need at any one time to be able to survive and the items they will need to carry alongside them. In the *Resident Evil* series, every weapon will always take up at minimum two spaces in the inventory: one for the weapon itself and at least one more for ammo. It is extremely easy to make inventory management frustrating, and there are some horror games that have no inventory, and the player can only hold one item at a time. Regardless of your intent when it comes to inventory, the UI for handling items should be easy to use to avoid frustration.

Being able to drop off items was a necessity for horror games. Going back to *Alone in the Dark*, the player could literally drop anything off anywhere in the environment. Later survival horror games would have storage spaces at save rooms or major checkpoints with the items stored showing up in any storage box. Another option is to not have any inventory or resource management which is typically seen in adventure-style horror games. The player can only pick-up items used for puzzles or opening doors and said items will be chosen automatically when the player reaches a relevant point.

There is no one perfect way to design a resource system for your game, as it will be dependent on the kind of gameplay you have, how challenging you want the game to be, and the enemies the player must face.

6.3 Enemy Design

The topic of enemy design, when applicable, will be in each *Game Design Deep Dive* entry, as every genre treats enemies differently. As an original offshoot from the action genre, enemy design is of huge importance for horror games as they are the elements that create the highest tension (Figure 6.6).

The basics of enemy design mirror action games by having a tier system of the enemies in a game. When ranking enemies, there is a common rule for how enemies are categorized by their tiers.

Figure 6.6

A horror game with good enemy design will create different ones to serve certain purposes or challenge the player in a specific way.

- **Tier 1** – The basic enemies that make up the bulk of encounters. They are never really a threat one-on-one but present a danger when swarming the player. They can be hard to fight at the start when there is a lack of strong weapons and ammo, but they will easily fall once the player finds a stronger weapon.
- **Tier 2** – Stronger enemies that are harder to kill. They will often shrug off the player's starting weapon and it may be safer to run away when they are first encountered. If the player can get better weapons, these enemies will eventually become easy to kill like the Tier 1s. Usually, Tier 2 enemy groups are smaller compared to tier 1 due to how hard it is to fight them.
- **Tier 3** – Support/specialty enemies. Enemies that are designed to supplement the other attacking enemies. By themselves they are quite easy to kill but can add difficulty when paired with the other ones. A common example would be enemies who stay in the back and attack at range while their close-ranged friends rush in. Enemies that are exclusive to a specific area or situation would also apply here. Their numbers are often kept small and are inserted into groups of the previous tiers.
- **Tier 4** – Bosses. Immensely powerful enemies who show up at specific points in the game. They are often required to be fought to move the story along or get a necessary item. Depending on the game, sometimes after the boss encounter, these enemies may show up in groups of the other tiers.

This tier list is just a basic example, and multiple enemies can occupy the same tier or extend the tier list depending on the game's design. For a practical example, here is the tier list for the original *Resident Evil*.

- **Tier 1** – Zombies. Slow moving enemies that attack the player in close range with acid vomit or grabbing and biting them. Can be killed in one hit in the head with the shotgun.

- **Tier 2** – Hunters, spiders. Hunters are fast moving enemies that perform jump attacks and swipe at the player with their claws. Spiders are medium speed enemies that throw poison which can infect the player.
- **Tier 3** – Crows, Cerberus dogs, bees, plant tendrils, and sharks. Crows show up as a group in several areas. They are not hard to kill but are hard to hit due to their speed and size. Cerberus are fast enemies who can attack by biting and pinning the player down and attack in packs. Bees show up for one area and do minor damage but can poison the player. Plant tendrils cannot be killed by the player's weapons and can only be avoided or use an item to kill them in a puzzle room. Sharks show up in one area and the player must run away and drain the water to deal with them.
- **Tier 4** – Yawn (giant snake), Plant 42, Black Tiger (giant spider), and Tyrant. Yawn shows up twice in the game and causes massive damage with bites. Plant 42 must be weakened by a puzzle before fighting and attacks with giant tendrils. Black Tiger is a larger, faster version of the normal spiders. Tyrant attacks with grabs and claw swipes and can run at the player. He is fought twice, with the second time requiring the rocket launcher to finish him.

When designing and placing enemies in the world, it is important to think about the player's options at a given time. A stronger enemy who outclasses the player can be used to gatekeep a section: preventing the player from going down that route until later. If you want the player to run away from a situation, you could have multiple enemies swarm that the player would not have the ammo possible to kill them all.

In most horror games, the player is not meant to kill every enemy, because either it would be too time-consuming or they do not have the resources to do that. One of the best examples of forcing the player to weigh the consequences of combat was in the *Resident Evil* 1 remake released in 2002. When a zombie was killed, if the head were not destroyed or the body set on fire, they would reanimate as "crimson head zombies." These zombies would be a higher tier of danger and elevated the dangers of combat at the start. Without stronger weapons, it was not possible to fight them safely. There is no limit to the creativity of enemy design in any game genre. Thinking outside of the norms can lead to unique encounters or memorable enemies. *Dead Space's* "necromorphs" were unique because they could only be killed by severing their limbs, as opposed to just shooting them in the head. Some games will allow the player to clear out an entire area of enemies to make it safe, while others will just **respawn** them over time to keep the player on their toes.

Some titles will have enemies or bosses with specific conditions on how to defeat or avoid it and have been referred to as "puzzle fights." Instead of being about using firepower, the player must use a specific item or the environment to get by them. In *Alone in the Dark*, there were several rooms where ghosts were set up. If the player tried to attack them or ran into them, they would turn into a tornado of fog that would chase the player and kill them instantly.

Deciding what attacks enemies use is another area where there is no limit from a design perspective. The amount of damage will need to be balanced based on

Figure 6.7

A good boss fight should be different from any previous encounter and require the player to figure out how to defeat it.

the player's ability to heal and the overall difficulty of the title. For many survival horror titles, enemies only had close range attacks. I feel this was done partly due to the constraints of the fixed camera system discussed in Section 4.3 and that long ranged attacks remove the horror to some extent. There is something about seeing a mob of monsters running towards the player that is lost when dealing with a few enemies standing back and opening fire on them.

Over the course of the last decade as indie developers experimented with combat-less horror games, the role and functionality of enemies changed. For titles where the player cannot fight, enemies are often able to kill the player in a few hits, or just one from a major threat. In the next section, I will talk about stealth gameplay, and stealth and enemy design go together for this part. Due to the lethality of the enemies, the focus on the design became how they track the player and how does the player survive an encounter. Even though the player cannot fight them directly, that does not mean they do not have options. Returning to the *Clock Tower* series, a major part of the design was using the environment to trap Scissorman and take him out of commission for a few minutes.

One final example of enemy design is having an enemy who actively tracks and hunts the player down and cannot be defeated like the other enemies. I have coined the term "Alpha Antagonist" to describe them, and I will discuss this further in Chapter 9.

As a developer, your goal with your enemies is to avoid designing something that can be figured out and mitigated easily if you want your game to remain scary. However, this is a short-term goal, because players will do everything they can to figure out your game. Even some of the hardest and scariest indie games released in the past decade have extensive guides and breakdowns of how to play them.

No matter how your enemies are designed from a gameplay perspective, coming up with unique character designs, stories, and if you can, voice acting can go a long way towards adding to the experience (Figure 6.7). There is a reason why

1980s horror is considered by fans to be an iconic period, as directors focused on making their villains interesting: Pinhead, the Tall Man, Freddy Kruger, Jason, and more. When I talk about the rise of indie horror in Chapter 8, part of the reason why the scene exploded was developers creating memorable villains, regardless of the mechanics themselves.

Ultimately, enemy design is where horror can really stand out compared to other genres. Having a unique or incredibly memorable villain has helped many indie games grow and gain notoriety, and I will discuss this point further in Chapter 8. Often, a popular enemy can also be used as part of the lore of the game as I discussed in Section 5.4. Remember this, no matter how creative an enemy or enemy type is, the more the player is exposed to them, the less frightening it comes. In Chapter 9, I will talk more about the pacing that you want in a good horror title, and why less is more.

6.4 Stealth Design

Stealth gameplay is its own genre and will hopefully be a later entry in the *Game Design Deep Dive* series, and stealth and horror are one of the most popular combinations to use. Stealth as a game system can make the player feel extraordinarily strong or incredibly weak depending on the context. Many action and tactical games use stealth as a way for the player to pick apart enemy groups one at a time or strike against a main target such as in the *Assassin's Creed* series (developed by Ubisoft and first released in 2007) or *Hitman* by IO Interactive (first released in 2006) (Figure 6.8). An advanced example of this would be the "predator mode" featured in the *Batman* series by Rocksteady which was first released in 2009. In it, the player was the most powerful character on the field and could stalk and defeat groups of enemies with all the advantages that Batman had.

Figure 6.8

Stealth can mean different things depending on the game – it could be used as a form of hiding, or to stalk a target, and how powerful the player feels will be based on the gameplay.

For this book, I am going to focus on the other side of stealth and how it is used to build tension and keep the player feeling helpless. Stealth design in all its forms starts with how the player is detected. Different designs will focus on certain metrics, with the two most popular ones being sight and sound.

Sight often works by programming a vision cone that each enemy has and is placed in front of them. Some games will have a two-tiered cone: an outer cone for noticing something is off and goes to investigate, and an inner one that instantly detects the player. Depending on the game and difficulty of the stealth, it is possible to walk into the outer cone and get away before the enemy notices something is off. Once the player is in the cone, they can either immediately trigger the enemy's response, or the enemy may give the player a chance to get out of sight. This is often represented by an alert meter that appears over an enemy: when the meter fills up, the enemy becomes alerted to the player.

Sound works by having objects and characters in the game that makes noise generate a kind of "sound echo." The range of the echo is determined based on how loud the noise was, and if it touches the enemy, they will be alerted. Unlike sight, sound echoes will go through walls (and sometimes floors) for enemies to hear. Some titles will just have any loud noise generated alert the enemies regardless of their actual position to it. The ranges for sight and sound to alert enemies can also be tweaked by having difficulty settings.

While sight and sound are the most popular, that does not mean you cannot get creative. Some games have used smell (and how the wind carries the smell). Advanced examples have used additional conditionals such as letting the player wear a disguise that lets them go to certain areas unnoticed. Just like with enemy design, feel free to get as creative as you want when coming up with your stealth system.

The other major element of stealth gameplay is how the player can avoid detection. The simplest option is to literally hide behind an object and peak around corners. Some games turn this into an actual mechanic: giving the player the option to lean up against an object and better conceal themselves. Series like *Thief* (developed by Looking Glass Studios and first released in 1998) and *Splinter Cell* (developed Ubisoft and released in 2002) had the lighting factor into how enemies detected the player. The darker it was, the closer the enemy had to be to see the player.

Being able to mitigate the player's presence is one of the cornerstones of stealth gameplay. Crouching down and walking has been used to conceal a player and reduce the noise of their footsteps. With the examples about lighting – destroying light sources or turning them off has been used. A popular option for avoiding detection has been the use of wardrobes or any environmental object that the player can hide in (Figure 6.9). While hiding, the player is invisible from enemy detection and is often used as a way of escaping from a pursuing enemy. Depending on how difficult the game is, designers may let enemies search hiding spots for the player.

While the point of stealth in horror design is to make the player feel helpless when directly facing an enemy, that does not mean the player cannot have

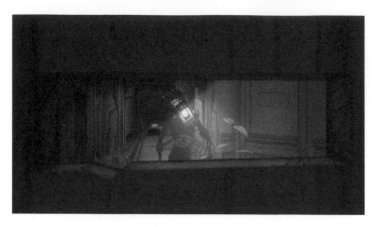

Figure 6.9

Having a dedicated spot for hiding from enemies has been a staple of a lot of horror games.

some advantage. Being able to create distractions that can lure the enemy away is a popular mechanic and gives the player some measure of control without it being too powerful. For games that try to straddle the line between action and horror, they may allow players to finish off enemies easily with a sneak attack or by using traps. The risk is that if the player slips up, they may not be able to defeat the enemy in a direct confrontation. With *Clock Tower*, the use of environmental traps was the only way to temporarily stop whoever was chasing after the player. If the stealth attack is too good with no risks of performing it, then the game just becomes another take on the power fantasy design I discussed in Section 6.1.

How you design the world and environment also plays a huge part. Wide areas with lots of obstacles to hide behind can make things easy. While narrow paths with very few rooms can lead to a tense experience. Some games are designed so that there are multiple options, while other ones may only have one correct route; again, this depends on the design and difficulty the developer wants.

Enemy design is another factor when it comes to stealth gameplay. In terms of stealth specifically, you need to think about the following variables.

1. What detection systems will the enemy use?
2. What range will the enemy detect the player?
3. How does the enemy search for the player?
4. How quickly does the enemy respond to the player?
5. What happens when the player is detected?
6. Can the enemy be killed?

To go over each point briefly, the detection systems have already been covered. For games that feature different enemy types, they may have enemies who only detect the player in one specific way: Someone who is blind but can hear well and another enemy who is the opposite. Another trick that has gained popularity was based off a monster featured on the hit BBC show *Doctor Who* with the weeping angels. The concept is that the enemy only moves or responds when the player is not looking directly at them, which creates a tense situation when the player is forced to look away to do something.

The range at which the enemy will be able to spot the player or be alerted comes down to how hard you want the game to be. Some stealth games, like the *Metal Gear Solid* series developed by Konami and Hideo Kojima (first released in 1998), would show the vision cone on the map. A smaller cone makes it easier for players to get around an enemy, and why most horror games will go with a long one.

For the third point, there are different **AI** systems that can be used. The common one is to program specific patrol patterns that each enemy will perform unless they detect the player. The patrol, or cycle, repeats on loop and is the easiest option. One issue with this system is that if the game is too linear; i.e., there is literally only one part of the cycle when the player can move unseen, it turns the game into an exercise of just performing the same action the same way to proceed.

An advanced example has the enemy searching in a general area. The enemy knows that the player is somewhere in the vicinity, but not the exact position, and they will wander randomly from room to room. For this system, there is no way as a player to specifically know where the enemy will go, and this can lead to cases where the enemy turns around or turns a corner when the player was not expecting them and get caught. When the player manages to escape, the enemy will often move to the next area in front of them to repeat the stealth in a different area. Another version of this is where the enemy will hunt the player and I will discuss this more in Chapter 9 with alpha antagonists (Figure 6.10).

As I talked about, enemies can be programmed to respond slower or faster depending on the overall difficulty of the game. Typically for horror, enemies will respond immediately upon detecting the player to keep the tension high. Returning to the topic of scripted events and triggers, having the enemy become alerted when the player picks up an important item or does something special is another trick to quickly raise the stakes.

A lot about the overall difficulty with stealth design comes from what happens when the player is detected. While chasing after the player is often the go-to response, there can be enemies that alert other ones to the player, with the most famous example being security cameras. With horror, the common response is for the enemy to give chase and depending on the design it may be possible to outrun or get away from them. For harder games, being spotted by an enemy may just automatically get the player killed by them.

When combat is involved, deciding on whether the player can kill, or at least temporarily stun, the enemy is a major decision. Giving the player the ability to permanently remove an enemy from the field is a powerful act and will remove tension in the game. Being able to stop them for a few minutes can create tension

Figure 6.10

The more reactive the enemy is to the player, the harder it becomes to sneak around and often leads to the game focusing on trial-and-error gameplay.

as the player will be thinking about how long until the enemy comes back and starts chasing them again. Depending on the resources involved can have a huge impact on difficulty, as I talked about with *Siren* in Chapter 2 and how there was no way to make an area safe and consuming resources was dangerous for long-term play.

Everything about how the player can (or cannot) deal with enemies and what each enemy adds to the experience will impact the horror and tension of your game. The goal is to give the player just enough options that they feel like they are the ones trying to survive, without limiting them so much that the game becomes a chore to play. As I discussed in Section 6.1 with the power fantasy, if the player cannot impact anything, then the game becomes a passive experience and loses its ability to generate horror.

Ultimately, the point of this chapter is that there is no one right way to design content for a horror game. Part of what led to the resurgence of horror among indie developers was rejecting the status quo from major companies and forging a new path away from what happened in the next chapter.

6.5 Puzzle Design

For the final point of this chapter, it is time to talk about puzzle design. Puzzles have been a part of the game industry since the rise of the adventure genre and to explore all aspects of it would be too much for this book. Returning to the original design of survival horror and being inspired by adventure games, puzzle gameplay was a major part of it (Figure 6.11).

Figure 6.11

The *Resident Evil* franchise has always used puzzles as a form of progression and gating where someone can explore from the start.

The function of puzzles in survival horror serves several purposes. The first and most common element is a way of reducing tension and breaking up the repetitive nature. Puzzles allow the player to focus on something other than being scared. Puzzles are also used as a form of progression that I will talk more about in Chapter 9. The general concept is that an obstacle or obstacles are keeping the player from moving to the next area, and they must figure out what is needed to get past them.

There is another book waiting to be written about the scope of puzzle design in videogames, but for my purpose, I want to quickly breakdown some of the overall concepts. Puzzles in games can be categorized for lack of a better term into "linear" or "nonlinear" puzzle designs. A linear puzzle means that there is a fixed number of solutions to the puzzle; usually one, but some developers may offer a few other ones based on the story or design. Another way of describing this kind is a "lock and key" puzzle, with that term coined by adventure game designer Ron Gilbert.

A nonlinear puzzle is when there is no set solution to the puzzle. While there is only one win condition, there are countless ways of getting to it. This is often seen in critical thinking-focused puzzles and programming-style puzzles. Instead of the focus being to solve the puzzle, these games generally turn into a contest of coming up with the most optimal or unique solution when compared to other solutions.

For horror, and the fact that horror is about creating a specific experience, designers will make use of lock and key design. Again, there is a lot that goes into designing puzzles for any genre that I do not have the space to get into here. The common rule is that the puzzle needs to fit the environment. With that said, that has not stopped developers from creating puzzles that make no logical sense given the situation, such as in the *Resident Evil* series. It was later retconned that all the environments in the early games were designed by an in-universe architect who specializes in traps and puzzles. How puzzles fit into the world and pacing of your game will be discussed more in Chapter 9.

For many developers starting out, puzzle design can be one of the hardest areas to tackle. If a puzzle is not designed right or is too difficult, it can completely stop the progression and kill any pacing in your game. Beware of designing puzzles that require outside knowledge to solve, such as knowing chemistry, reading musical notes, and history. For challenging puzzles, it is considered good etiquette to not allow enemies in the same room as the puzzle to let the player focus only on it. Everything the player needs to solve a puzzle should be in the game itself. For horror specifically, a good puzzle should be interesting enough that the player should be happy to solve it, but not so commanding that everything else comes to a halt. I have played games where one annoying puzzle takes me out of the experience and is often the point that I stop playing it.

This is where playtesting must be done to figure out how someone responds to a puzzle. One of the problems that led to the falling out of the adventure genre for mainstream audiences was an escalating trend of overly complicated puzzle design. Where the only way someone could figure it out was to purchase a strategy guide or get help from someone else. Many modern adventure games and horror titles have tone down the difficulty and complexity of their puzzles (Figure 6.12). With that said, some took this a little too far and led the genre almost to its downfall.

Figure 6.12

A "puzzle boss" is when the player needs to figure out how to either damage the boss or perform some action that would be the finishing blow and, in a way, is an example of an environmental puzzle.

6. Creating Scary Gameplay

7

The "Death" of Horror

Figure 7.1

Resident Evil 4 redefined horror and began the period of action horror design.

DOI: 10.1201/9781003199250-7

7.1 The Reinvention of *Resident Evil*

Back in Chapter 3, I discussed how *Resident Evil* would go on to become the foundation of horror and defined it for almost a decade. In 2005, the series would redefine horror, for good and bad, with *Resident Evil 4* (Figure 7.1). The history of *Resident Evil 4* is as interesting as the final product. With each game in the series, the development team tried to push in a new direction. When it came to *Resident Evil 4*, the developers had a problem with deciding on where to take it. Their previous main entry *Resident Evil Code Veronica* released in 2000 was positively reviewed and considered one of the must-have games for the Sega Dreamcast. Likewise, the prequel *Resident Evil Zero* and the *Resident Evil 1* remake, both released in 2002, were also highly regarded for the time.

For this entry, the game went through four completely different takes before arriving at the version released. One iteration was more action-focused and downplayed much of the horror in terms of creating a powerful protagonist. The team behind it would eventually redesign the story and transform it into the award-winning *Devil May Cry* franchise first released in 2001. The other three iterations each told a different story and tried to add in more supernatural elements while retaining the survival horror gameplay.

Finally, Shinji Mikami took over as director and ordered a complete redesign of the game. One of the major points was getting rid of the fixed camera systems and tank-like control scheme that the previous games made famous. The philosophy was to rebuild the franchise and get away from the older design and structure. *Resident Evil 4* starred the protagonist of *Resident Evil 2*: Leon Kennedy. Now working for the government, he is tasked with finding and saving the president's daughter who has been kidnapped somewhere in Europe.

Instead of fighting zombies, players had to deal with townspeople who were infected with a parasite known as "Las Plagas." Where zombies were slow moving and could only attack by biting (or spitting acid), the enemies of *Resident Evil 4* could use weapons, dodge attacks, and even run at the player. One of the most dangerous enemies wielded a chainsaw and could kill the player in a single hit if they got too close. The game also featured several boss fights, including another famous enemy "El Gigante" that was a massive ogre-like enemy. One of the best designed enemies for survival horror showed up in the final action-packed part of the game in the form of "regenerators." These slow-moving enemies could not be killed by traditional weapon fire, as they would regenerate any bullet-based damage done to them. The only way to put them down was to use a sniper rifle with a modified scope to pick off the Las Plagas parasites in their body or used grenades while they slowly lurched towards the player.

To compensate for the increased lethality of the enemies, the ability to control Leon was improved. *Resident Evil 4* would popularize the "over-the-shoulder" or behind the back camera style which is a variation of the third-person camera system (Figure 7.2). A third-person camera typically shows the view of the game behind and slightly below the character model. This keeps the player's character in the middle of the screen and can be spun around and altered. The shoulder system keeps the camera closer to the player, which is more atmospheric and reduces their vision. When aiming, the character model is placed on either the left- or right-hand side of the screen to not obstruct the player's targeting. As an important UI element, modern-day games regardless of genre will allow the player to shift which side the character model goes to when aiming.

Instead of only being able to change the facing or angle of their character when aiming, *Resident Evil 4* introduced full targeting and location-based damage. Shooting an enemy in their legs could cause them to stagger or fall allowing the player to run right by. Headshots did the most damage and could set up enemies for follow-up attacks. The use of headshots became a tough choice with later enemies wearing faceplates and armor to protect them. There was also the chance that shooting an enemy in the head would cause the parasite to become hostile with new attacks. It was even possible to shoot the weapons out of enemy hands or attack them at different elevations.

For the first time in a horror game, the player had the most control over their inventory which was laid out as a giant suitcase. Items could be rearranged and moved around like tetromino pieces, and the case could be expanded by purchasing upgrades.

Given the amount of work that went into designing it and the previous iterations, there were some oddities left in. The game introduced the character known as "the merchant" who became a popular meme that sells the players new weapons and upgrades existing equipment. There is no explanation about this character, why he is here to help Leon, and how he just shows up all throughout the game. Speaking of the game, the tone and pacing of *Resident Evil 4* feels like it is three smaller games. The first third takes place in a village and surrounding

Figure 7.2

By switching to the over-the-shoulder targeting system, it made it far more easier to fight groups of enemies and provided compensation for the increased number of them.

countryside and plays the closest to the horror of previous titles. The middle is in a European style castle that throws all manner of death traps and wacky contraptions at the player. The final part is on a military island with the player fighting soldiers with plenty of explosions.

Despite these nitpicks, *Resident Evil 4* would go on to become one of, if not the most, popular game in the franchise and one of the greatest videogames ever made. At that time, no franchise did such a top-to-bottom redesign of its gameplay that successfully, not even when games transitioned from 2D to 3D. This success was not lost on Capcom and would go on to frame future *Resident Evil* games until the main series crashed in 2012 (Figure 7.3).

Without realizing it then, *Resident Evil 4* would be the game that officially began the trend of action horror design that I will discuss more in Section 7.3. The use of the over-the-shoulder camera would also become popularized by third-person shooters and many action games going forward.

With that said, horror fans began to feel betrayed by Capcom and the growing focus on action horror. The atmosphere, pacing, and puzzle solving of previous games were replaced with a greater focus on action movie staples, explosions, martial arts fighting, and more explosions. Even though *Resident Evil 5* and *Resident Evil 6* released in 2009 and 2012, respectively, were not bad games, they had little horror design to them. The number of enemies the players fought continued to be upped, and the player's ability to fight and avoid was greater refined. In *Resident Evil 6*, it was possible to dodge around attacks and perform wrestling-styled takedowns on the undead. There was a greater focus on **coop** play, with both 5 and 6 designed and balanced around either having an AI partner or playing with a friend. Unfortunately, the AI was limited in terms of the utility it would provide and could not perform advanced maneuvers. This added

Figure 7.3

Even elements like the quick time event-driven fight shown here were considered ahead of its time as the first examples, before they would be repeated ad nauseam in other games.

7. The "Death" of Horror

increased difficulty as online architecture wasn't really established the way it is today until at least the mid-2010s.

Resident Evil 6 began a 5-year lull for the main franchise, but Capcom continued to experiment with spinoff titles. There were three different series done by different teams: *Resident Evil Revelations* released in 2012 by Capcom, *Resident Evil Operation Raccoon City* developed by Slant Six Games in 2012, and *Umbrella Corps* also developed internally by Capcom and released in 2016. Of the spinoffs, *Resident Evil Revelations 2* released in 2015 came the closest to the survival horror aesthetics of the originals in my opinion. In Section 7.4, I will talk more about the trend of action-horror led to the phasing out of the genre among AAA developers.

While *Resident Evil* began an unfortunate decline, another series came out that would follow the same trajectory, but faster.

7.2 Dead Space

As I mentioned earlier, *Dead Space* was designed by Visceral Games and was positioned to be a competitor to Capcom's *Resident Evil 4* as the goal by EA who published the series. Taking place in the far-future, players control an engineer named Isaac Clarke who is part of a rescue team to the ship his wife is on, the Ishimura. Once there, he discovers the ship has been infected because of a structure called "the marker" that drives people insane and revives corpses as monsters called necromorphs. From an art standpoint, *Dead Space* was one of the best-looking horror games for its time and beat *Resident Evil 4* in that department. The necromorph design was similar in terms of body horror to the movie, *John Carpenter's The Thing*, with bodies twisted and contorted into non-human

Figure 7.4

Dead Space featured some of the most unique enemy designs the horror genre has ever had with the necromorphs, and how just blindly firing on them wasn't going to kill them without limb shots.

shapes. To distinguish it from other horror games, necromorphs could only be killed by severing the limbs as opposed to the standard attacks to the head in the genre (Figure 7.4).

Another defining point the series had was its use of a **diegetic** UI that represented the operating system built into Isaac's suit. His "rig" would holographically display his inventory, highlight important areas, show him where to go, and display his health as a bar on the back of his armor. The sci-fi theme would extend into his weapons and abilities. Each weapon had different usages, and everything could be upgraded using acquired power nodes hidden throughout the game. Early on the player is given the power of stasis that lets them slow down objects and enemies. Because precise hits were needed to attack limbs, this power proved to be highly effective.

The series featured puzzles that were built into the environment. Often, Isaac had to move objects around to open doors or power on machinery. Besides stasis, the player could pick up objects and throw them around. In *Dead Space 2*, this also provided an offensive option of picking up the claws from killed necromorphs and launching them at other enemies. Several areas required the player to slow down objects using stasis to get through safely. Since the game took place in space, there were many sections that required the player to go into areas with no oxygen and/or low gravity to fight and explore.

Despite the accolades from critics and fans, EA put pressure on Visceral to earn more money with the series. While the second game was in the same style as the first, the third game released in 2013 was more action focused (Figure 7.5). Not only was combat faster, but players could team up for coop play. Microtransactions were put in as an option to buy better weapons and have a greater advantage with this practice becoming a criticism of EA and other AAA companies.

Figure 7.5

By the third main entry, the series began to mirror *Resident Evil* with a focus on action and coop play over survival horror.

In 2012, it was reported that EA demanded that *Dead Space 3* must sell at least 5 million copies to justify continuing the series. To put that into perspective, *Resident Evil 4* has been reported selling just over 10 million copies worldwide by 2020: 15 years after its release. When everything was said and done, the game sold around 605,000 copies which was impressive for the genre, but not enough to keep it going. Despite that, *Dead Space* did get spun off into other games, comics, and an animated movie. EA was trying to do what other horror developers and publishers were aiming for – making a bigger and more profitable *Resident Evil*. Unfortunately, that did not work out and I will talk about that more in Section 7.5.

7.3 Action Horror Design

I will not be spending as long on action horror design compared to survival horror earlier in this book. The reason is that many of the mechanics and systems of action horror are shared by action games in which the action genre will be a focus on a future *Game Design Deep Dive* entry. That sharing of design led to the falling out of the genre by major studios.

The principal factor that separates action horror from survival horror is a greater focus on player progression and a growing power curve (Figure 7.6). Survival horror typically spaces out new weapon upgrades and tries to keep the player limited in terms of their resources. Action horror will often quickly give the player access to a wide assortment of options for killing enemies. The focus of the experience is more about the player fighting ever increasingly dangerous waves of enemies.

In a typical survival horror game, the player must often decide to fight enemies now or run away and try to deal with them later (or if ever). Action horror

Figure 7.6

Action horror gameplay is often more akin to an action movie aesthetic, rather than horror, with a consistent focus on escalation instead of controlling the tension.

design will often make use of the arena encounter format seen in action games: trapping the player in a singular area until all the enemies are killed. This sets up the problem I laid out in the previous chapter about enemy design: the more the player is forced to fight and get used to enemies, the less scary the game becomes. With the later *Resident Evil* titles, I was killing more enemies in 5 and 6 than I did in the first three games combined.

What makes survival horror, horror, is that the player should not want to be fighting enemies: either they are too much of a resource drain, too dangerous to fight, or there are ways of getting around them. Action horror focuses on the combat, and in a way, brings the game closer to being a power fantasy which should be avoided. You can certainly have boss fights in survival horror, which force the player into an encounter they cannot escape from, but those should be the only times that happens.

Speaking about power, action horror tends to allow the player to upgrade their characters using in-game resources. This can include, but not limited to, more ammo capacity, more health, more stamina for running, doing more damage, taking less damage, and even unlocking special skills that can be used to make the game easier. By the end of an action horror game, the player's character will often by far be more powerful and capable than they were at the start, which goes against the philosophies of horror I laid out in Chapter 5. If there are any upgrades in survival horror, they will either supplement what the player has, like inventory upgrades, or give them a new option, such as a new weapon, but they will not fundamentally change how that character behaves. The focus on power gives the player control over the situation and lets them know that whatever is thrown at them, they will be able to kill it. Action horror games still used many of the same tricks as survival horror such as jump scares, but often are lacking in terms of long-term play.

Before I go on, I want to bring up an important point. Everything that I said in this section comes off as largely negative, but action horror games are still well-designed titles, many of them earning accolades and being well-received. As I will discuss in Section 7.5, the problem came down to developers trying to earn new fans while burning their old ones.

7.4 A Snapshot of Action-Horror Games

Resident Evil and *Dead Space* may have been the biggest names, but there were several notable other examples of games that also kept the action horror trend going. The first-person shooter genre had many horror-themed games released throughout the 1990s and early 2000s, but despite that, none of them had as big of an impact on the market and horror design compared to *Resident Evil 4*.

One of the most famous series was *System Shock* released in 1994 by Looking Glass Studios. The game was praised for its mature plot, use of environmental storytelling, and a compelling villain in the form of the AI: Shodan. Players had

Figure 7.7

Clive Barker's Undying was the first time the veteran director worked on a game project and voiced one of the characters.

to fend off enemies while searching for resources and figure out what is happening. The series would go on to have another game released in 1999 and be the inspiration for the *Bioshock* series developed by Irrational games (first released in 2007). What is interesting from a design standpoint is that the Shock series were more about shooter design than horror but used horror themes to create a dangerous atmosphere. In Chapter 9, I will elaborate more on having a horror theme in non-horror titles.

In 2001, EA Los Angeles teamed up with famed director Clive Barker for the game *Clive Barker's Undying* (Figure 7.7). The story followed a man named Patrick Galloway who has been summoned by a long-time friend Jeremiah Covenant to help him. The Covenant family has been cursed and have come back to life as monsters at the estate, and only Patrick can fight them. *Undying* was unique from other action horror and first-person shooters for the time besides having *Clive Barker* as a part of the project. Even though the game did focus on combat, there were a variety of dangerous enemies who would resist different attacks. Players could use traditional firearms along with spells that could be upgraded, and the UI was set up that they could use one of each type at any time.

The world design was chapter-based with parts of the estate accessible from the start and more unlocked as the game progressed. The story was paced with Patrick going after each member of the family one at a time, following clues and eventually fighting them, before returning to the estate that acted as the hub. While the game did become a cult classic, it did not sell well enough for EA to greenlight a sequel. Following *Undying*, Clive Barker produced another game: *Jericho*, which was heavily criticized for poor gameplay.

Despite the cult classic status, there has only been one licensed game based off *John Carpener's The Thing. The Thing* was released in 2002 and developed by

Computer Artworks. The game was played as a third-person shooter and was pitched as a sequel to the movie. The plot dealt with another group finding the destroyed Antarctica base and having to fight the Thing and people disguised as it. The unique mechanic was keeping people alive and trusting you, while not over committing and giving your resources to someone infected. Unfortunately, the rest of the mechanics were on the basic side, and the game often just played as a standard third-person shooter.

Before *Dead Space* would define action horror in the west, *The Suffering* was released in 2004 by Surreal Software. Unlike *Resident Evil 4* that used an over-the-shoulder camera, *The Suffering* used one of the older versions of the behind-the-back style: placing the camera behind and slightly above the character so that they would be framed along the bottom of the screen. The story involved a convict named Torque who has been incarcerated for murdering his family, when he arrives at the prison, the place is attacked by demons and he is forced to fight his way out and figure out what truly happened. Besides using traditional guns, Torque could also transform into a monster which would eliminate any tension or horror. The game's story and setting were praised for being different from other games, with every enemy type based off a form of execution. The series got a sequel in 2005 with *The Suffering: Ties that Bind*, which was more action-focused and the last game in the series.

Doom 3 (again, released in 2005) may have been the third game in the popular trilogy, but the developers decided to experiment with going a more horror route. (Figure 7.8) When compared to the first two, and even later entries, it is the slowest game. The story was a remake of the original *Doom* this time told from a horror perspective. In the first version, players had to constantly switch between their flashlight and weapons to see and shoot, respectively. Instead of running through

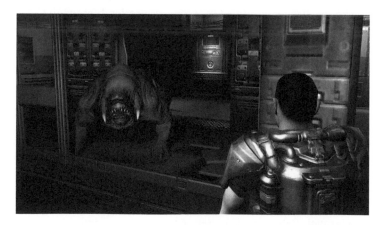

Figure 7.8

Doom 3 was ambitious for its time with trying to create a horror experience for the franchise but felt like a game caught between two different masters.

levels, players had to take their time as the game was full of monster closets and liked to spawn enemies behind them.

The problem that *Doom 3* had was that the design and combat was clearly built off the older, more arcade-like, design of the first two, but the developers wanted to slow that down to try horror. This was akin to being given a Porsche, but the car has been locked to only go 10 miles/hour. The game was eventually re-released as the *Doom 3: BFG Edition*, which placed the flashlight on the player and removed the need to ever switch. The overall look and feel did not help matters, with the **gunplay** being dull and environmental design very generic. *Doom 3* did end up getting an expansion but would lead to ID software doing a third reboot and succeeding with *Doom* 2016.

I already spoke about *Condemned Criminal Origins* released in 2005 in the previous chapter, but it was one of the best action horror games released that decade (Figure 7.9). Of the games in this chapter, it is the only one that truly had combat best suited for horror. The focus on close-range using objects as improvised weapons gave it a gritty feel. Unlike other action horror titles that would escalate fights with more enemies, *Condemned* only did that rarely and instead focused on making individual fights stand out. The environmental design focused on decrepit buildings with lots of open space and paths for enemies to ambush the player.

One of the best areas in the game was the penultimate level that tasked the player to hunt down clues in a farmhouse. The clues could be tackled in any order, and enemies would appear after progress was made. The atmosphere of the abandoned house coupled with the freedom to explore made it an amazing set piece for horror. The sequel had a similar level that took place in a large cabin with enemies so quiet that they could sneak up on the player.

The success earned the series one more game *Condemned: Bloodshot* released in 2008. While it reviewed respectively, as with a lot of horror franchises, the second game tried to expand the story and stakes with more action and confusing plot points. For fans, while the second game had deeper mechanics, the theme and pacing of the first one was better.

2014 was an interesting year for horror, as it marked the decline of horror in the AAA space and would be remembered as one of the major moments for indie horror that I will come back to in Chapter 8. Following his departure from Capcom, Shinji Mikami formed a new studio Tango Gameworks and would create *The Evil Within*. The story followed detective Sebastian Castellanos who after investigating a murder spree at a hospital is knocked out and awakens in a nightmarish world. The gameplay follows the previously established *Resident Evil 4* formula in terms of combat and controls with a few exceptions. Enemies could only be killed permanently by burning them or destroying their head. Unlike *Resident Evil 4*, players could upgrade Sebastian using "green goo" found throughout the world. There was a sequel *The Evil Within 2* released in 2017 that was focused on open-world horror, a topic I will talk more about in Chapter 9.

Figure 7.9

Condemned Criminal Origins is one of the few melee-focused action horror games, and it still holds up in terms of aesthetics and gameplay.

The last game I will talk about for this section is an important one. Another classic horror movie franchise was *Alien*, and there have been many games based off the property going back to the 1980s. With few exceptions, the games based off *Alien* were average to poor, but 2014 would give fans one of the best takes with *Alien Isolation* developed by Creative Assembly. The story was a sequel to the original film, with the player controlling Ripley's daughter Amanda who is trying to find out what happened to her mother after the events of the first film. Arriving at the station the Sevastopol, Amanda discovers the place is in anarchy and a Xenomorph is on the loose. The game was praised for its survival horror design with a focus on sneaking around and crafting items to get passed enemies. While the player could fight, any conflict risked attracting the attention of the Xenomorph. This is the game where the concept of an alpha antagonist came from, and there has not been a game since to take it to this level of danger.

The Xenomorph was designed around two different AI systems. The first one gave it the general location and area of where the player was at, while the second one made it search for the player and set up traps. If the xenomorph grabbed the player, it was an instant kill and forced them to reload the game. Speaking of loading, *Alien Isolation* introduced tension by requiring the player to wait several seconds to activate a save machine to save their progress, which the Xenomorph could interrupt and kill them. The game has been highly praised for its use of the IP, but at this time, there are no plans for a sequel.

This section went over some of the major names of action horror, but I hope you noticed a trend with this list. As time went on, fewer action horror games were being released. Publishers were having a hard time rationalizing spending money on developing a new horror game, and they learned a harsh lesson about the action horror market.

7. The "Death" of Horror

7.5 How Did Horror Die

The horror genre, much like platformers, never really died in the sense that it disappeared completely, but there was this sentiment among major studios that the genre was no longer viable to keep making games in. So much of this discussion is framed around the success of *Resident Evil 4* and what it meant for the genre. The philosophy of action horror design is the explicit goal to try and create a horror game that is also marketed towards action fans (Figure 7.10).

Therefore, many of the action horror titles released following *Resident Evil 4* focused on action game elements: coop and multiplayer design, microtransactions for additional content and making the game easier, and a far faster-pace of gameplay to keep the player constantly engaged. These elements also meant a higher budget that publishers expected these new games to earn back...and then some. The industry was taking note of the success of franchises like *Call of Duty* and *Battlefield* in terms of retaining players and earning money. *Call of Duty* was originally released in 2003 by Infinity Ward but did not achieve its major success until 2007s *Call of Duty Modern Warfare* which brought an entirely redesigned multiplayer experience. Since then, the series has had multiple sequels released by different studios. *Battlefield* was first released in 2002 by DICE and always focused on huge multiplayer battles.

Talking further about the designs of these series would be off topic for this book, but the success was not lost on the rest of the industry. In 2012, the director of *Resident Evil Revelations 1* Masachika Kawata gave an interview talking about his thoughts on survival horror and where it needed to go:

Figure 7.10

This is one of the most infamous moments in *Resident Evil*, and horror genre history, and "Chris punching a boulder" is often compared to "jumping the shark" as when something goes too far off the rails.

Especially for the North American market, I think the series needs to head in that [action-oriented] direction,

Looking at the marketing data [for survival horror games]... the market is small, compared to the number of units *Call of Duty* and all those action games sell,

A "survival horror" *Resident Evil* doesn't seem like it'd be able to sell those kind of numbers.[1]

The problem with this sentiment is that horror no matter what is still niche, especially when put next to something like *Call of Duty*. There has only been one horror game that has managed to be multiplayer-focused and has financially succeeded, and I will discuss it in Chapter 9.

In Chapter 10, I will be discussing the market viability of horror in more detail, but the challenge of creating a good horror game is that the better you are at generating terror, the harder it will be to get more people interested in playing it. Fans of genres expect certain design elements when they are buying a game; if a game does not have it, they are going to feel cheated and return it if possible.

Even the best, and highest rated, horror games released only have a fraction of the fanbase compared to major franchises in other genres. The one outlier of a franchise that still maintained success with lots of copies sold was *Resident Evil*. Again, there is only a finite number of people out there who want to experience something scary. The goal of action horror was to try and have it both ways: create a game that is scary but gives the player the power to fight back. Trying to make a game that appeals to hardcore action fans and hardcore horror fans ended up in the situation of the falling out of the horror genre. If someone wants to play an action- or shooter-based game, examples like *Battlefield* and *Call of Duty* are the more attractive option. Besides that, it is easier to support long-term play of games like that, where the pacing of horror does not work as well, and I will talk more about that in Chapter 9. For horror fans, they did not want to play a game that was only about combat, and they did not buy those games (Figure 7.11).

The final point is about the cost of designing these games. At the AAA level, publishers expect huge profits based on the amount of money spent creating these games. Going back to *Dead Space 3* and EA expecting the game to sell 5 million copies, there was no way a horror game was going to earn that in a short period of time. The production costs at AAA studios are always considerably higher compared to indie developers, with every game must be earning a return on that investment. As the cost of game development increased, horror games were simply not going to make as much money compared to other genres no matter how much was sunk into development. However, this once again paved the way for indie developers to keep horror alive by focusing on design over graphics, and with a drastically smaller overhead.

---

[1] https://www.gamasutra.com/view/news/167135/Survival_horror_market_too_small_for_Resident_Evil_says_Capcom_producer.php.

Figure 7.11

The Evil Within at the time was a breath of fresh air for horror fans, as the closest to *Resident Evil 4*'s slower focus – yet still action – horror design.

8

The New Horror

Figure 8.1

Outlast made it clear that the player had no power in the world and could only hide or be killed by the inmates of the asylum.

DOI: 10.1201/9781003199250-8

8.1 Stealth Horror

In the last chapter, I spoke about how horror was beginning to wind down in the early 2010s from major studios. During this time, the burgeoning indie developer space began to expand. Back in Chapter 6, I talked about different approaches to avoiding the power fantasy when it came to horror and how indie developers began to embrace the concept of removing the player's ability to defend themselves (Figure 8.1).

The first two examples I talked about: *Amnesia the Dark Descent* and *Outlast* showed that there was a market for horror without a focus on combat. There was never an official genre title given to games like this, but for my purpose with this book, I will use the term "stealth horror." Unlike survival horror where players could fight back, stealth horror is all about avoidance with puzzle solving sometimes as a secondary system. Stealth gameplay is a complicated design, as I discussed in Chapter 6, and the fact that players could never fight back against the enemies chasing them became immensely popular.

A trend that you will see in this chapter is how one successful take on horror led to the creation of many games basing their designs off it, and there are numerous examples to discuss in Section 8.3. Even though many games did copy the design systems, everyone was doing their own take off them which led to a variety of titles.

In 2014, consumers saw the possibility of reigniting horror from AAA studios when the demo for the game *P.T.* was released by Konami. The game started another horror trend with the idea of the infinite loop scenario. The player was trapped in a home that as they walked through the hallways, they would loop back to where they began. After a few cycles, the home started to twist and distort, and there were puzzles that showed up that had to be solved to move on to the next loop. Besides the creepy atmosphere, the player was also menaced by a ghost that would appear randomly to scare them, but the player was never in any danger.

Finishing the demo required solving one final riddle that involved hunting down symbols in specific spots. The reward was the reveal that *P.T.* was going to be *Silent Hills* that I talked about in Chapter 3. Unfortunately, the falling out between Hideo Kojima and Konami ended that plan (Figure 8.2).

Stealth horror design has several popular styles that many indie games copied, and I will discuss that along with examples in Section 8.3. The general concept is a game of cat and mouse: with the player's job to complete a task while avoiding whatever is after them. As I discussed in Section 6.1, the problem with just relying on stealth and nothing else is that it usually limits the number of ways of succeeding. Depending on the complexity of the AI, it could either track the player no matter how much noise they are making, or the player could run circles around it if the detection range were too small.

The examples that worked would add in a secondary system or gameplay to do while sneaking around, such as finding the items to solve a puzzle or a key to get

Figure 8.2

P.T. may have been short, but it delivered on its concept of an infinite loop scenario perfectly, and to this day, people still try to imagine what *Silent Hills* could have been like as a full game.

out of the area. The worse examples would have long periods of time of exploring with no checkpoints, and the player must follow one exact route to avoid the detection of the enemy. Returning to the topic of trigger events from Section 4.5, some developers will have the enemy automatically detect the player after they complete a specific event no matter how stealthy they were from anywhere on the map. This can be viewed as a cheap shot by the developer.

There are benefits to stealth horror. Removing the player's ability to fight back, but still requiring them to accomplish goals, can be a great way of raising tension. What consumers saw over the 2010s was developers exploring every possible avenue for stealth horror in, and there is one game that truly signaled the rise of the indie horror scene and became the template for so much indie horror.

8.2 *The Five Nights at Freddy's* Phenomenon

Indie horror for the most part has been a niche success with very few breaking into the mainstream, with one exception. *Five Nights at Freddy's* is arguably one of the most recognizable properties to come out of the 2010s. First released in 2014 and developed by Scott Cawthon, *FNAF* told the story of a security guard for a Chuckie Cheese like restaurant called Freddy Fazbear's Pizza. The player's job is to watch the restaurant during the late-night shift until 6 am under the guise of keeping it safe. Instead, something is wrong with the animatronics who move around the restaurant and kill you if they reach you (Figure 8.3).

The game's minimalist design kept the player in one room: the security station. Your only options are to watch the monitors to see where the animatronics were at any moment and turn left or right to view the doors leading in, light the corridors, and close the doors. From a production standpoint, *FNAF* was

Figure 8.3

Five Night's at Freddy's is a perfect example of how the elements of horror can be done correctly without needing a huge budget.

incredibly light compared to other examples of horror, and Scott had a brilliant idea to keep costs down and horror high.

There are no animations rendered during a play of *FNAF*. Everything occurs either off screen or as a prerecorded animation. The game would check whenever the player stops watching the monitors or shifts their viewpoint to see if an animatronic has "got them." When that happens, the player is treated to a high-pitched jump scare of the animatronic surprising them before a fade to static indicating they are dead.

The AI, which would grow more complicated over the franchise and had different rules for each animatronic. With each in-game night that passes, the speed and aggression of the animatronics would increase, and more animatronics would show up. Players were forced into a game of micromanagement, as they had to check monitors, shine their flashlight to see if someone was close, close doors, and watch for surprises, all while their overall power ticked down. Not only did the player have to keep themselves alive but running out of power would lead to Freddy automatically attacking them in the dark. The wildcard factor in the original *FNAF* was the Foxy animatronic who would respond based on how often the player used the camera. If Foxy leaves its room, the player only had a few seconds to close the door before it rushes into the room and kills them.

FNAF is one of those indie games that came out at the perfect time and hit all the right notes to become a success. Thanks to the focus on jump scares, it was an excellent game for streamers and youtubers to play and react to, which got the word out about it. It was this focus on games aimed at influencers that would become a major marketing aspect of indie games, and the horror genre was the perfect fit. The characters themselves, all based off animatronics that kids and parents would recognize, were immediately relatable and became iconic. The final part of the game's success was the lore and mystery built up around it.

To explain the lore of the series at this point could easily fill a book, and there have been several books written on it with original stories. Each game expands on the mystery surrounding the pizzeria, why the animatronics are like this, and gruesome events that may have led to everything happening. Speaking of books, the series has been licensed out with everything from original fan stories, toys, and fan games, and there have been talks for years now of having a *FNAF* movie. The fan games have been an interesting prospect, with Scott working with developers and giving his blessing for people to create games based off the series and characters. Some of them play just like the *FNAF* games, while others use the characters in different designs.

From a design standpoint, *FNAF* is brilliantly simplistic. The gameplay is easy to understand by anyone, the stakes are avoiding a scare, and the lower production values improve the game's tension. Because the player can only look at specific angles, it sets them up for jump scare events any time they move the screen. Later games would add in new animatronics that had their own rules, additional things to juggle, and ways of hiding from specific animatronics. The limited gameplay has also made the series very port-friendly, with a VR version, mobile game, and even spinoffs by Scott.

As the design evolved, so has the number of things the player must juggle or examine (Figure 8.4). Later entries would introduce places with multiple rooms, alternate endings based on meeting specific conditions, and master-level challenges. The AI was programmed with different "threat levels" ranging from 1 to 20. The higher the number, the quicker and more frequent that specific animatronic would attack. The hardest challenge in any *FNAF* game is often referred to as a "20/X/" challenge (X being the number of 20s that represent the animatronics in a game).

Figure 8.4

The series' roster has grown considerably, with each game introducing new iconic characters with their own rules and behaviors.

At the time of writing this book, there are officially seven main games in the franchise from Scott, but given the number of fan games out there, it is hard to get an accurate number of just how many games are in the *FNAF* property.

Without realizing it at the time, *FNAF* would become a foundation of indie horror. With that said, there are some design criticisms I have about the franchise. The structure of the game is highly linear due to the lack of control on the player's part. The heart of the game is the AI that governs the behaviors of the animatronics. However, the AI patterns can be figured out and exploited, which limits the organic nature of survival horror. As the lore surrounding the series grew, so did the amount of work needed to experience it. The fanbase has examined every inch of each game to find secrets and more plot points to connect everything, and some of these aspects are so hidden that most players may never find them all. When the difficulty goes up, it does not change anything that the player is doing, but simply restricting how someone plays the game to only the most optimal strategy. Winning at the highest difficulty often is about figuring out the one exact pattern that works and repeating it for how many minutes required.

With that said, there is no denying that the *FNAF* formula has worked, and the combination of scares, lore, and iconic characters led to it becoming a sensation. Games like *FNAF*, *Outlast*, and *Amnesia* set the stage for a renaissance of horror completely divorced from AAA studios.

8.3 The Variety of Indie Terror

To catalogue every major horror game released in the indie space is borderline impossible thanks to the sheer number of them put on smaller stores or just sold from their respective game sites. I am going to attempt to name some of the larger design examples and notable games that were developed, but even that may not accurately list all the ones out there (Figure 8.5).

For as long as there have been popular PC games, there have been **mods** in all shapes and sizes made for them. Over the years, there have been modders that made horror stories that used the assets of a game when making their own "game within a game" in a manner of speaking or known as a "partial conversion mod." One of the first I experienced was *They Hunger* which was a mod for *Half Life* (created by Valve and released in 1998). The mod was created by Black Hunger Games and released in 1999. The game played exactly as *Half Life* did in terms of the core gameplay loop but focused on limiting the player's weapons and put them into scarier situations. *Half Life* and its sequel have been the foundation for many mods that sometimes would be turned into their own games. In 2013, one of those games was released called *Cry of Fear* developed by Team Psykskallar. At this time, there are modders making original games based off the original *Resident Evil* trilogy and remixed harder versions.

As I said, games like *Amnesia* and *FNAF* would set the standard for most indie horror templates in terms of removing the player's ability to fight back against

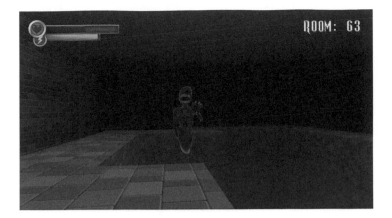

Figure 8.5

Indie horror was not limited to any specific art style, aesthetic, or gameplay and has done a lot to show that there was still life in the genre.

enemies. One of the more popular design examples required the player to perform a series of tasks while one or more enemies is stalking them. The player is limited to sneaking around and sometimes being able to run for a limited duration. As the game progressed, more tasks are added for the player to complete while the overall aggression (or number of enemies) increased. The first one of this type was the game based off the urban myth about "Slenderman" and was called *Slender: The Eight Pages* released in 2012 by Parsec Productions.

One of the early examples of indie horror was *Lone Survivor* released in 2012 by Jasper Byrne. The game achieved cult status thanks to being one of the first indie horror games to focus on psychological horror. The main character is trapped in a city after a plague wiped everyone out, and they must scavenge for resources while solving the many puzzles to get out. What made *Lone Survivor* stand out was that the story would change based on the decisions by the player, and if they would take specific drugs which caused the main character to hallucinate.

Pixel art has been one of the go-to art styles by indie developers over the 2010s and, despite the low fidelity of the art compared to modern graphics, can still be used to generate horror if the atmosphere and tension are on point. Besides *Lone Survivor*, another good example of doing a lot with a simple aesthetic would be *the Last Door* released by the Game Kitchen in 2014. The entire game used simple pixel art to create an impressive atmosphere for its Lovecraftian story. Unlike most of the games in this section, *the Last Door* was an adventure game and was focused entirely on the story and puzzle solving as opposed to direct combat.

Another popular angle for indie horror was basing it off situations and people not normally used in a game. In 2015, *Among the Sleep* was released by Krillbite Studio and told the story from the perspective of a toddler. Players explored the toddler's dreams and had to control a character who could barely walk and tried to solve puzzles while avoiding a mysterious monster after them.

Figure 8.6

Horror in the mid-2010s began to experiment with all different kinds of scenarios, and even games inspired by other ones still went out of their way to be its own unique experience.

Just as there have been many fan games based off *FNAF*, so have there been games that tried to capitalize on a similar formula by taking a toy or something not supposed to be scary and ratcheting it up to horrific levels. *Tattletale* developed by Waygetter Electronics and released in 2016 used a toy like the 1990s sensation "Furby" (Figure 8.6). Players had to care for the toy to keep it docile while performing tasks, or it would attract the attention of its mother who would kill the player if it got too close.

Another example was *Bendy and the Ink Machine* released in 2017 by Joey Drew Studios. Instead of toys, the game used character designs meant to emulate the golden age of animation. Like *FNAF*, a lot of the popularity came from the unique characters and the lore about what happened. Unlike some of the other games listed here, players did get weapons and could fight back at certain times, but these were often limited to specific combat sections. The bulk of the gameplay focused on exploring the remains of an animation studio, solving puzzles, and avoiding a powerful monster who could kill the player.

In terms of *Amnesia*'s style and storytelling, the studio Bloober Team has made a name for themselves with their titles that mirror certain aspects. Starting from *Layers of Fear* released in 2016, each game has the player moving from area to area solving puzzles in creepy environments. The art and graphical fidelity have been some of the best examples from the indie space. Each game is played in a chapter format and has multiple endings based on what the player does at specific points. They have been criticized for focusing almost entirely on jump scares as the only form of horror.

Another popular style are games that start off without any clue that they would be horror, oftentimes using cartoon graphics and a calm atmosphere to disarm the player. At some point, the shoe drops, and the player is confronted with something scary. Some games would even completely change the gameplay when the mood shifts to further add to the tension. These games became popular among youtubers as a way of reacting to the calm before the storm and then the results after.

One of the first examples was the game *Spooky's Jump Scare Mansion* originally released in 2014 by Albino Moose Games. The game began with the player exploring a cartoony mansion where the jump scares were just cute cutouts of characters. As the game went on, players would start to encounter monsters or "specimens" that would track them from room to room and try to kill them.

Another twist game was *Pony Island* released in 2016 by Daniel Mullins Game (Figure 8.7). The game introduces you to playing the game within the game called *Pony Island*, but as you play and unlock more elements, disturbing sights and sounds start to appear and the player learns that they are communicating with the devil.

Doki Doki Literature Club just released in 2017 by Team Salvato was a visual novel game that began with the player joining a book club ran by an eccentric cast of high school girls. What starts as a typical dating story, reveals fourth wall breaking disturbing images and conversations along with an ending that I will not spoil here.

Baldi's Basics first released in 2018 by Basically Games used the concept of "edutainment" or using videogames and other entertainment mediums to educate kids. The game's aesthetic was a low-budget education game from the 1990s, with the initial goal to solve basic math problems in a weird school. Quickly, the player is forced to run for their lives as Baldi begins to chase them, and the only way out is to solve all the math problems in the game.

As I mentioned, each popular horror game would go on to inspire other developers to create their own versions. With that said, there have been a few horror games to come out that either have not been fully copied or just stand as a unique concept. *Darkwood* developed by Acid Wizard Studio and released in 2017 was an open-world horror game where players had to complete a goal in procedurally generated spaces. The setup was that there were important areas, or points of interest, whose position would be different each time someone started a new game. Players needed to gather resources and upgrade their equipment while setting up defenses for the nighttime; when they had to hunker down in their base and wait until morning. Even though the general path through the game remained the same, where players had to go and what hazards would appear at night were different. There was a great feeling of having that "last stand" moment waiting each night for whatever threats to come that has not really been replicated since.

Procedural generation has been used more and more in horror design in the back half of the 2010s. By using content generation, it has afforded developers to create experiences that are not 100% the same each time and keeps the player in the dark longer. Many horror games that use procedural generation in this regard often feel like "horror roguelikes." For more about roguelike design, you can read my third book *Game Design Deep Dive: Roguelikes*.

Figure 8.7

Trick games like *Pony Island* were more about being unsettling than full-on horror, but still delivered a different experience from other games.

One example of a horror roguelike would be *World of Horror* developed by Panstasz that uses the imagery and aesthetic from Junji Ito while telling stories with randomized situations and events. At the time of writing this book, the game is still on early access with no estimated date of release.

Lost in Vivo released in 2018 by Kira used claustrophobia to generate additional horror and tension (Figure 8.8). The player is trying to rescue their service dog after it was pulled into the sewers. The game used a low field of view to simulate the feeling of the walls and environment oppressing the player. With the use of combat and puzzle solving, *Lost in Vivo* felt the closest to being a survival horror-designed title that I saw from the indie space in some time. The psychological themes and broken down/disgusting aesthetic reminded fans of the *Silent Hill* series. From a graphical standpoint, *Lost in Vivo* looked like an early 3D game much like the PlayStation era. During the late 2010s, developers began to use early 3D as the basis for their games in the same way that pixel art was used in the early 2010s.

Yuppie Psycho released in 2019 by Baroque Decay featured an original premise for survival horror by combining the horrors of monsters with the horror of starting your first day at a corporate job. Instead of having direct combat, players had to sneak around enemies while looking for clues and the next part of a quest chain. Even without direct combat, there were still fights with bosses that were handled more like puzzle fights. The goal is to figure out how to hurt or get around the boss before it can kill you. This is also one of the longer horror games from the indie space, featuring different endings and paths through it.

The use of full motion video, or FMV graphics, has seen a resurgence in the 2010s by indie developers, and in 2020, the game *At Dead of Night* was released by

Baggy Cat Ltd. The entire game is played as a full motion movie with the player moving through the environment one scene at a time. The goal is to solve the mysteries of murder victims at a hotel by the current caretaker Jimmy. There are no rendered animations like *Five Nights at Freddy's*, as the game will check if the player has been caught and will play a jump scare when that happens. The core gameplay is about finding clues in the hotel and reaching specific spots to watch short scenes about the victims and questioning their ghosts for answers. All the while, Jimmy is tracking the player across the different floors and will knock them out if they are caught.

Faith currently in development with a planned release in 2021 by Airdorf Games is another example of how aesthetics and tension can elevate older art styles and graphics. The entire game is done using 8-bit graphics and sets up its atmosphere perfectly with little music and haunting sound effects and cutscenes to increase the tension. As an added detail, the game uses voice synthesizers to add to the scare factor.

Another popular trend was the rise of multiplayer horror out of the indie scene, but I will be talking more about the examples and design of it in Section 9.1. For this section, multiplayer horror typically focuses on a group of players either having to fend off or avoid an AI enemy, or having a player control the monster who is stalking the group of humans.

In Section 5.5, I mentioned how the growth of public game engines influenced the fidelity of graphics for indie developers. The use of these engines has also afforded many developers the chance of just telling a unique story and gave rise to the concept of microhorror.

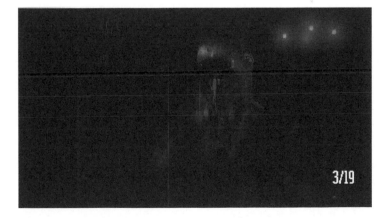

3/19

Figure 8.8

Some of the better examples of indie horror purposely used lower quality graphics as part of the horror and mood, such as the less detailed, but still disturbing, enemies of *Lost in Vivo*.

8.4 Microhorror

Because horror is more about theme and storytelling as opposed to game mechanics, it has provided a lot of opportunities to tell unique stories or do something nontraditional. An exceedingly popular avenue for indie developers has been the concept of making a "microgame" as a way of exploring one unique concept in a short time span. Microgames can be anywhere from a few minutes long to at most around an hour. For something that is entirely story-driven, a microgame provides the developer a way of telling the story exactly how they want, without having to worry about the mechanics or length getting in the way (Figure 8.9).

When it comes to horror, microhorror is the complete antithesis to AAA horror and the problems that plagued it that I talked about in the last chapter. This is also why it is hard to provide a complete listing of horror games from the indie space due to the sheer number of microgames in it. The indie storefront "Itch.io" has been one of the best places for developers to put up all varieties of games and where a lot of these microhorror games have been posted.

The beauty of microhorror has been allowing developers to experiment with a unique concept that may not be deep enough for a full-length game. There have been horror games built around driving, cooking, sleeping, golf, and dating, and I am sure just about any topic you could come up with. In a way, microhorror is a good analog to anthology series like *The Twilight Zone* or *Tales from the Crypt*. Each episode is self-contained and explores one topic, and the story is wrapped up by the end of the show.

One example of the potential has been the games developed by the studio Puppet Combo. Their aesthetic has been combining the early 3D graphics style I mentioned last section, with the tone of a 1970s/1980s slasher film. At the time of

Figure 8.9

Microhorror can explore concepts and stories at the most basic level and is akin to short vignettes.

writing this book, most of their games are available on Itch, but they have started to bring them to other stores with the first one being *Murderhouse*.

While many indie developers have used engines like Unity and Unreal for horror, the story-driven nature of horror has given developers another option with the engine RPG Maker. The RPG Maker series is an engine and toolset designed around the explicit purpose of making games in the 16-bit top-down style of RPGs from the late 1980s/early 1990s era. The number of games made using the RPG Maker engine is exhaustive with many first-time developers using it.

The disadvantage when it comes to microhorror from a market perspective is that these games are in a way a niche within a niche. Due to their smaller size and reach, many of them are not known outside their hardcore fans. This also presents a problem when it comes to pricing them on a store. The horror genre is already a tough market, but a game that is only designed for less than an hour's worth of content becomes harder to justify a purchase. To combat this, many microhorror developers will either release it for free or make their games on the difficult side, adding time to the game due to difficulty and trying to figure out how to survive. The one advantage this way is that given the smaller scope and development time, the revenue needed to generate a profit is drastically lower compared to AAA or other indie horror games.

Another option that came about during 2020 was having a compilation of titles bundled together. The *Dread X Collections* are published by Dread XP as a space for horror designers to experiment with microgames (Figure 8.10). Each collection is a bundle of these titles framed around a specific theme and finished under a short time frame. The result is a collection of games that could not be further apart in terms of design, quality, aesthetics, and art, but put together as a

Figure 8.10

Micro horror may not be for everybody, especially if you're looking for a fleshed-out game, and collections can be all over the place in terms of content and quality.

more attractive package compared to being sold separately With the popularity of the *Dread X* collections, Dread XP is using them as a springboard to publish larger horror games. Another collection that is out and gaining popularity is the "Haunted PS1 Demo Disc." Released exclusively on Itch.Io, the 2020 and 2021 collections are all designed to emulate the look and feel of PlayStation 1 era titles while raising awareness for new games. With that said, the collections still face a problem in terms of reaching a larger audience, but that discussion is more about marketing and not a focus of this book.

A microgame is a great way to experiment with a concept with as little risk as possible when it comes to development. If the idea fails, at least the investment was not that big. And if it does succeed, then the developer can either add more content or think about creating a bigger version of the game. Several micro-, or smaller, games have been re-released as larger games with more content or quality of life features.

8.5 The Revival of *Resident Evil*

Following *Resident Evil 6*, the focus on action horror was not bringing in the revenue Capcom was hoping for and the main series was put on hold. There were several multiplayer- and single player-focused entries released. While they did respectable numbers, *Resident Evil* as a franchise was falling out of relevance when it came to horror. In 2016, Capcom began to tease word that a new main entry was in development and using a brand-new game engine: the "RE Engine." Initial screenshots showed that the game was played in first person, and there were no mentions of any of the plot or lore of the existing games.

In 2017, *Resident Evil 7* was released and was both a return to form for horror for the franchise and a step forward with new design (Figure 8.11). Starring newcomer

Figure 8.11

Resident Evil 7 surprised everyone with how it felt like yet another fresh start for the franchise, and the popularity of the Baker family as the major threat of the game.

8. The New Horror

Ethan, the story followed his investigation to find his missing wife who had turned up after three years in Louisiana. Upon arriving, he is captured by the Baker family and held hostage on their estate. The first-person perspective drew similarities to *Outlast* and *P.T.*, which the developers used to great effect with jump scares. Like the older titles, *Resident Evil 7* had combat with different guns, but players could also mitigate damage with carefully timed blocks reducing it further.

There were two distinct groups of enemies in the game. Replacing zombies were creatures called molded that would move around inconsistently and had to have their head destroyed to finish them. There were only a few types of molded each with their own attacks. The Baker family were alpha antagonists that would roam their respective areas and give chase if they saw Ethan. The only way to deal with them permanently was during boss fights. Puzzle solving returned in a far smaller fashion, with a greater focus on searching for resources and items in the detailed environment.

Even though the game was still more focused on action compared to the originals, critics and fans praised it as a new beginning for the franchise. Following *Resident Evil 7*, Capcom released remakes of *Resident Evil 2* and *Resident Evil 3* in 2019 and 2020, respectively. Using an updated version of the RE Engine, both games were played with the over the shoulder style camera. The two main innovations had to do with enemy design. Zombies were updated to have their movement completely affected by momentum and how damage was done to them. Shots to the leg can temporarily stun or knock a zombie to the ground. As a zombie is hit, the body will react and affect how they move towards the player. For the first time in the series, zombies could move between rooms in real time and follow the player around.

Resident Evil 2 also brought back the character "Mr. X" as an alpha antagonist who would show up after specific events and chase the player down (Figure 8.12).

Figure 8.12

For many fans, the *Resident Evil 2* remake was the first time they saw Mr. X, as he originally only showed up in the B-Side run and was just one of the many improvements that made it a great game.

Unlike the Baker family, Mr. X would roam throughout the area until specific events would remove him from play. Players could temporarily knock him down, but he would get up again after about a minute of inaction.

While most horror games did feature difficulty settings to let players make the game easier or harder, *Resident Evil 7* and the *Resident Evil 3* remake had their highest difficulties remix the game compared to the lower settings. Enemies and item placements were shuffled around and required a different path through. *Resident Evil 2* used the same format of having an A and B route for both characters, with the B route shuffling up item placements and puzzle solutions.

As far as remakes go, *Resident Evil 2* was considered the superior one compared to 3 which was criticized for removing a lot of the areas and content that were in the original In 2021, *Resident Evil Village* was released which continued the story laid out in *Resident Evil 7*. Instead of just one area, the game took place in an entire fictional European village. Many fans and critics pointed similarities to *Resident Evil 4* with both the setting, and the ability for players to upgrade Ethan and his weapons. For now, *Resident Evil* as a franchise is back, and there have been rumors of remaking the other games in the series besides working on new entries.

9

Complex Horror

Figure 9.1

Multiplayer horror, at this time, only explores a few distinct areas, but the potential is there with each new experience.

DOI: 10.1201/9781003199250-9

9.1 Multiplayer Horror

For the final design chapter of this book, I want to focus on some advanced forms of horror games and design. For the longest time, there has been this sentiment that multiplayer and horror cannot work, and why very few games up until the 2010s experimented with it. One of the early examples of a game that did this loosely was *Resident Evil Zero* released in 2002; however, that game was about one player controlling two different characters. The first major example would come with *Resident Evil Outbreak* first released in 2003 and allowed groups of players to try and survive in the *Resident Evil* universe.

The problem when it came to multiplayer was simply having a second similar character to share in all the content. Having someone to provide equal back-up and assist with all the combat greatly removes the tension of playing. If you are playing with friends, it is easy to be more concerned about playing with them than anything scary going on. This was part of the action horror trend that began in 2005 and coop became a major feature. Being able to play with a friend has led to a variety of modes in action games, including the popular zombie modes that have been featured throughout the *Call of Duty* series.

When indie horror introduced the idea of having gameplay without combat, this opened the door for having multiplayer where players must work together to survive instead of fight (Figure 9.1). In the last chapter, I briefly mentioned some of the more popular design examples that I want to expand on now, starting with players against the monster.

Cooperative games have grown in popularity over the last decade thanks to better online architecture providing access to high-speed internet to a larger population. What used to be something resigned only to local plays with someone next to you, it is possible to play a game with someone from almost anywhere in the entire world. Multiplayer design is way too big of a field to talk about now and would be something saved for a future *Game Design Deep Dive*.

For this design, a group of players must team up to either figure out how to destroy a monster or survive long enough to escape. The monster in question is controlled by the AI that will do anything it can to stop and take out the players. Depending on the design, it may be possible to temporarily stop the monster or distract it, but other than winning the game, there is usually no way to kill it. Some games allow other players to rescue defeated ones, or once a player is killed, they are removed from the game.

Part of the beauty of cooperative design is creating challenges that require the players to work together. This can be done by having obstacles that require two or more players to do something to get by it or having **asymmetrical balance** with each character bringing a unique role to the team. To keep these games replayable, designers will often randomize where essential items or goals are, or even change what monster is attacking the player on each play of the game. Because communication is key, many of these games will have built in voice chat, but to add to the immersion, voice chat can be set to only work localized based on where characters are in the environment.

This design architype has been used by many indie games released over the last decade, but unfortunately, a lot of those games are no longer in service. Part of the problem with multiplayer in any format is the fact that if the community around the game moves on, these games can become unplayable without full groups for the remaining players. Like traditional horror, the problem with long-term play is that it is hard to keep players scared once they know what to expect. After a few games, the game becomes less about the horror and mood, and more about winning the match. Once that happens, unless the game has enough content and is consistently updated, people will not stick around to just repeat the same exact playthroughs. The concept of continual development of a game or "games as a service" didn't become a major trend until the 2010s and, even then, required a huge investment by the developer and publisher to make it work.

At the time of writing this book, one of the most popular examples of this specific design is the game *Phasmophobia* developed by Kinetic Games and still in early access at this moment (Figure 9.2). A team of four players must investigate randomly generate homes and figure out what ghost is haunting it before they are killed. The team must work together exploring the home and setting up devices, while looking out for each other and avoiding the ghost.

The other example of multiplayer horror is where a player becomes the monster that is hunting the other players. This kind of design is more advanced because both the monster and the people being hunted must have different advantages.

Figure 9.2

Cooperative gameplay pairs nicely with horror when everyone is on the same page about being scared and defenseless.

Like the previous example, the monster is usually not able to be stopped for long, and the survivors are typically trying to complete a task while getting around it.

There are several advantages to this style over the previous. Due to the monster being controlled by a player, it removes the need to create an AI that controls it. The absolute best AI-controlled characters still are limited by how they are programmed; a human player is far more reactive which pairs nicely with this kind of game. Due to a human controlling the monster, it affords the developers the chance to get more creative with unique abilities that would prove to be difficult to program an AI to use properly. Having players compete against each other is a form of user generated content that can greatly extend the lifespan of a game.

The disadvantage is that everything about the experience hinges on the skill disparity between the monster and the hunted players. If the monster player is just starting out, it can become frustrating to play with people who know all the best tactics that come with experience; the same can happen if the skill levels are reversed. This is often why games that feature competitive or ranked play will have a matchmaking system to keep similar skill levels together.

The current top example of this design is the game *Dead by Daylight*, released in 2016 by Behavior Interactive Inc. The game has earned its longevity thanks to an ever-increasing amount of lore surrounding what is pulling the strings in the universe, and frequent updates that introduce new killers and survivors. The game has also received multiple collaborations between iconic series and has featured killers like Michael Myers from *Halloween*, Freddy Kruger from *A Nightmare on Elm Street,* and more.

The gameplay tasks the four survivors to find and operate generators in a randomly generated space to open the exit doors and get out while the killer is stalking them. The survivors are not able to attack the killer but can drop pallets to temporarily stun them and do their best to dodge the killer. If they are spotted, they must try to outmaneuver the killer to get away; hopefully while their friends are repairing generators. If someone is caught, the killer places them on a nearby hook to sacrifice them. The hooked player can be rescued, but if they are hooked enough times, they will be automatically killed. Each killer has unique abilities and advantages to track and attack the other players. Over the years, the game has been enhanced with an upgrade system that allows players to upgrade the killer and survivor characters and adds **customization** to the gameplay.

Multiplayer horror is a concept that I feel still has a lot of room to grow and experiment, but there are some considerations with that. First, trying to directly compete with a similar game that is already out will often end badly for the studio. Regarding *Dead by Daylight*, there was competition with *Friday the 13th the Game* released in 2017 by Gun Media (Figure 9.3). However, a lack of updates and issues with the license has left the game stuck in limbo for years now.

As I discussed, multiplayer in any form lives or dies based on maintaining and growing its community. Once a multiplayer game begins to churn players, it becomes hard to grow that fanbase back. For developers who make it with any unique multiplayer design, the rewards can outweigh the risks as evidence by

Figure 9.3

Multiplayer horror, as with any multiplayer title, relies on continued content and support to remain relevant. Once *Friday the 13th* started to lose fans and had lawsuit-related issues, it was not able to get out of the downward spiral.

the games that blow up. There is a greater discussion to be had about the use of microtransactions in multiplayer games and their role in influencing someone to spend money, but that is beyond the scope of this book.

9.2 Open-World Horror

Horror for the longest time has relied on a tightly constructed experience when it comes to controlling the tension and pacing. In Section 4.5, I discussed the use of trigger events when it came to creating a structure for the game. Open-world design has grown exceedingly popular over the last 10 years and, with the power of game engines today, is no longer limited to only AAA studios like Bethesda. Using procedural generation, it is possible to create massive game spaces for players to roam around in (Figure 9.4).

Open-world horror is an interesting aspect of the genre, as it replaces the controlled buildup and release of tension with a general feel of unease with moments where things spike. There are not as many examples of open-world horror out there due to the complexity and challenge of the design. The most popular example is pairing open-world horror with survival mechanics. This works well due to the tension that is generated trying to survive and throwing in enemies and hazards to mess up someone's plans.

One of the first major examples of this design was the mod *DayZ* for the *Arma* series developed by Bohemia Interactive and first released in 2006. The series has always focused on realistic military combat and tactics. The *DayZ* mod that was introduced added in the idea of surviving during a zombie apocalypse while still having that attention to detail and complexity of combat. The mod proved to be

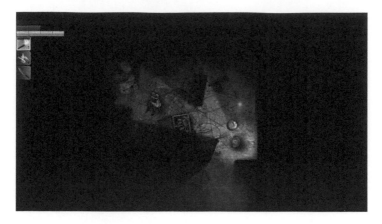

Figure 9.4

Open-world horror is less structured than traditional horror, making scares more surprising, but oftentimes inconsistent and harder to pull off.

so popular that Bohemia hired the modder to turn it into a full game that was originally released in 2018.

Titles like *The Forest* (released in 2018 by Endnight Games Ltd) and *7 Days to Die* (still in early access at this moment and developed by The Fun Pimps) (Figure 9.5) explore the concept of surviving in an open world under the threat of zombie attacks. Players must survive while gathering resources, crafting new gear and structures, and fending off frequent attacks.

State of Decay first released in 2015 by Undead Labs is structured more like a typical open-world game, but with the added challenge of building up a settlement and fending off the undead. Players need to explore the map to find points of interest that either hold supplies or destroy hives that spawn the undead. Each **NPC** they recruit can either tend to the settlement or go out with them to explore.

While not zombie-related, the game *The Long Dark* by Hinterland Studio Inc (first released in 2017) delivered similar feelings of tension and dread. Players must try to survive in a frozen wilderness by scavenging for supplies and avoiding the local wildlife. Just because they are not undead does not mean bears and wolves cannot scare an inattentive player just the same.

Open-world design is its own genre that could be covered in a future *Game Design Deep Dive*, but the basic attraction to it is the idea of exploring a massive gamespace at the player's discretion. Progression is usually handled in two ways: leveling up their character to unlock new abilities or things to do and finding better and new equipment that allows the player to push farther than before. As mentioned with titles like *Dark Wood* and *State of Decay*, progress is framed around completing set objectives or reaching points of interest. For survival games, progress is about getting specific gear or finding the resources needed to make essential upgrades. Due to the size of the space, open-world gameplay lasts far longer than what a traditional horror game could do.

The major difference once again is how the tension and pacing of the experience works. As a developer, you are trading in a finely tuned experience for one that is less controllable. Many open-world games today will have an AI that dictates what enemies do even when the player is not around; this has been described as an "A-Life" system by developers. Enemies can hunt for the player, fight other groups, move around at their leisure, and more. Oftentimes, an open-world horror game can be two different experiences. The first is the general exploration and survival portion, where the focus is less on combat and more about trying to get resources to survive. Second is when the player is forced to confront a specific event or point of interest that is more defined and linear.

The problem with this focus is that open-world games are typically full of a lot of wasted time moving from one point of interest to the next. During that time, the tension may disappear and be replaced with boredom or frustration. Despite having the word "survival" in the title, survival horror games typically do not focus on this level of detail in terms of survival. Depending on the gameplay, it may be possible for a player to become so comfortable that nothing will be able to bother them. Astute players can often figure out the best way of surviving and, when paired with superior gear, may no longer have any reason to be scared. This is also why the starting hours in these games are often the scariest and hardest to play.

This can be conflated if the game allows the player to unlock new abilities over the course of play. *The Evil Within 2* released in 2017 traded in the chapter format for an open world one. The player still had access to the same basic gameplay, but they were free to explore a destroyed town gathering resources and completing side objectives. Just like the first one, they could use the green goo to upgrade Sebastian and unlock abilities that made the game easier. The first quarter of the game is noticeably harder before the player gets those essential upgrades that give them more flexibility to fight and explore.

The problem when combining open-world design, either survival-based or not, with horror, is that the horror aspect does not last as long as the rest of the game. I have yet to see any game that tries this combination that can maintain the horror pacing and tension for anywhere near the same number of hours as the rest of the experience. Even if the player restarts, the limitation of open-world design is that there is often a fixed path of progression that is required to play regardless of if the world is procedurally generated. Returning to the topic of only having one shot at horror from Section 5.6, once the player knows what to expect, the horror aspect will fade away and all that is left is the survival.

Some developers get around this by having the bulk of the game focus on the survival or action gameplay, while having areas that slow things down and create a source of tension. In *S.T.A.L.K.E.R: Shadow of Chernobyl*, developed by GSC Game World in 2007, the game took place in an alternate version of Chernobyl after another nuclear disaster turned the place into "the zone." Players had to fight bandits, military forces, mutants, and overcome anomalies that affected the world to regain their memories. The bulk of the game took place in open

Figure 9.5

To try and keep scaring the player despite their progression, many survival games will escalate their threats over time. In *7 Days to Die,* the longer someone plays, stronger and more diverse zombies will appear.

environments, where it was often easy to spot enemies and engage them. At several points in the game, the player had to go into bunkers and underground tunnels and the mood changed. Underground, it was claustrophobic, hard to see more than a few feet in front without night vision, and more dangerous mutants would attack the player. Nothing about the player's abilities changed, but simply changing the environment and situation around them would generate horror for a few minutes at a time.

9.3 Alpha Antagonist

Throughout this book, I have referenced the concept of an alpha antagonist in horror design, and I want to explore it in more detail now. The difference between having an alpha antagonist and just having an unkillable enemy is that the alpha antagonist is an ever-present threat that intersects with the rest of the game experience that must be mitigated (Figure 9.6).

Looking at games like *Outlast* and *Amnesia*, the enemies are designed to only exist in specific areas and follow fixed patrol patterns. The player's focus is on avoiding them and nothing else; often if the player is detected, the game is over. With examples of alpha antagonists, the player is usually juggling other things, trying to get through an area, fight minor enemies, gather resources, etc. and must either fend off or avoid the alpha antagonist.

In the *Resident Evil 2* remake, once Mr. X is on the field, he is actively moving through the police station either chasing the player or trying to find them. His very presence raises the tension and difficulty, because the player knows that trying to fight other enemies or solve puzzles becomes a lot harder if he is in the

Figure 9.6

Alpha Antagonist work best when they are unpredictable, disrupting the player's plans, and force the player to adapt when they appear.

same room. Near the end of the game during Leon's campaign, Mr. X comes after the player while trying to dodge dangerous plant zombies.

Another consideration is giving the player a way to temporarily disable the alpha antagonist. It is often good to give the player the option early, but some games may delay it to increase the difficulty. In *Alien Isolation*, the Xenomorph can only be scared away by the flamethrower, but the weapon is not introduced until after several hours of sneaking around. With Mr. X, if the player has a weapon, they can attempt to knock him down for about a minute, but that is often a waste of resources. The decision to try and take on the alpha antagonist can be further muddled by having specific rewards or items drop for fighting them. In both *Resident Evil 3* and the *Resident Evil 3* remake, each time Nemesis is disabled outside of boss fights, he will drop a rare item or weapon.

With regard to difficulty when designing an alpha antagonist, there are several areas where things can be adjusted to raise or lower the difficulty of dealing with them. The first point is an obvious one: What happens if it catches the player? In both the *Resident Evil 2* and *3* remakes, getting attacked by Mr. X or Nemesis will result in damage, but the player can still recover. Mr. X does have a kill move when he grabs the player which can only be countered by using a sub-weapon. Once Mr. X has given chase, if the character is running, he will not be able to catch them. In *Alien Isolation*, the second the Xenomorph reaches the player or sees them the game is over.

The second point is whether the antagonist can be disabled or scared away. This point is dependent on the kind of design you are aiming for. If there is no hope of stopping it, like *Alien Isolation*, then the encounter always ends the same way. However, if it is too easy to do it, then the antagonist is no longer a threat. This is also why the flamethrower that could scare the alien was not introduced until further in the game as a form of a reward for surviving that far and was limited in terms of ammo.

The third point is what separates alpha antagonists from other enemies: how do they track and hunt the player? As I mentioned, unlike traditional enemies, alpha antagonists must be programmed to track the player and act as a secondary obstacle. This will be dependent on how your game space is laid out in terms of design and progression.

In *Alien Isolation*, each major area of the ship is rendered and accessible one at a time. When the player uses the tram to go to a new area, the game loads that area. What that means is that the Xenomorph is not literally exploring the entire game space to find the player. As I talked about in Section 7.4, the game makes use of two AI systems for the Xenomorph. The first one knows exactly where the player is currently and will send the Xenomorph to that specific level. The second one is the tracking AI that is used to tell the Xenomorph how to hunt and track the player but does not give it the exact location.

As the developer, you will need to figure out how attentive the alpha antagonist should be and how it detects the player. Going back to Section 6.4 with stealth design and detection, this will determine the overall difficulty of getting around the alpha antagonist. It can break immersion if the AI is so attentive that it knows where the player is without any warning or clue. During my time with *Alien Isolation* on the harder difficulties, the Xenomorph despite not seeing or hear me would stay in my general location or followed me as I moved around. For many games that feature an alpha antagonist, or just an enemy that hunts the player, it is typical when putting in multiple difficulty settings to adjust the AI's ability to detect the player based on the setting. In the game *White Day: A Labyrinth Named School* first released in 2001 by Sonnori Corp., players are chased by the janitor while exploring the different school buildings. On the highest setting, the janitor can hear movement up to several floors above or below the janitor.

With the example of Mr. X from the *Resident Evil 2* remake, the game never stops to load in a new area (I do not know if there is any loading done in the background) and instead restricts him based on the path through the game. Once Mr. X is active, he will roam the entirety of the main areas of the police station but will not go into the garage area. Once the player leaves the garage and moves into the back half of the game in the sewers, Mr. X becomes inactive again. He only shows up one additional time in Leon's campaign, and never again in Claire's. For the most part, he will search on his own for the player, picking up one key item does tend to trigger him to go after the player, but the AI for tracking is not as attentive as the Xenomorph's. Running or shooting enemies will tend to alert him, but he will not hang around an area the same way as the Xenomorph. If the player gets far enough away from Mr. X and does not run, it is possible for him to temporarily lose the player, but any loud noise (like gunfire) will alert him once again.

The final difficulty point is an important one for a game's design: is the alpha antagonist able to go everywhere? Depending on the experience you want for the player, this fact can dramatically raise the difficulty of a game. In

Figure 9.7

What held Nemesis back (and to some extent Mr. X) is that their interactions and appearances are fixed events, and can be easily countered by knowing when they show up and their triggers.

both the *Resident Evil 2* and 3 remakes, Mr. X, Nemesis, and any enemy cannot enter saferooms or any area where there is a typewriter set up for saving a game (Figure 9.7). If something is chasing the player, they will be stopped by an invisible wall that prevents them from going forward. While this does break the immersion, this is often done to give players a place to safely hide and collect their thoughts. Enemies are also forbidden from entering rooms where there are puzzles for the player to solve, to give the player a chance to focus on the puzzle solving.

In *Alien Isolation* as I talked about, nowhere is safe for the player. The only exception is during specific story events or areas where the Xenomorph will not go; everywhere else is fair game. There are also many indie horror games where the gameplay boils down to just outwitting the alpha antagonist in a large environment. Two of Puppet Combo's games are just that: *Stay out of the House* and *Nun Massacre* both released in 2018. Both titles are about exploring a building looking for items to solve puzzles and staying out of sight of a killer trying to catch you.

An interesting mechanic that I saw for the first time in *Stay out of the House* is that while the killer cannot enter the vent system to chase the player, if they spot the player escaping into one, they can turn on poison gas to flush them out and randomly place bear traps to catch the player.

The use of an alpha antagonist is an effective way of taking control away from the player in terms of an opponent that they cannot ignore or directly deal with. The more of a presence it has on the rest of the gameplay, the better it will be in terms of generating horror. If you can make their appearance and behavior unpredictable, it can keep the player in a constant state of confusion and terror.

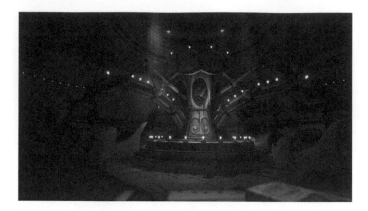

Figure 9.8

Horror gameplay is often built around specific sections or memorable situations as opposed to the obstacle course nature of platformers. Here, this boss fight breaks up the normal gameplay and closes out a section of hunting down power levers to turn on.

9.4 Pacing and Progression

Pacing and progression are essential elements of any videogame, and this discussion will often end up in every *Game Design Deep Dive*. The basic rule when it comes to the length of any game is that it should only be if the mechanics can justify the time spent. In *Game Design Deep Dive: Platformers*, the number of ways you could challenge the player with platforming obstacles dictated the length of each stage and by extension the game itself.

As I have discussed throughout this book, horror is more about theme than it is mechanics, which makes things a lot trickier to break down. The longer any horror property is, the harder it becomes to generate and maintain tension. As videogames grew lengthier, it became worse for horror designers who had to find ways to keep players scared after hours of play. A lot of horror games tend to run out of momentum by the back half of their playthrough.

To this day, there has not been one horror game that has managed to keep control over the tension and remain scary from beginning to end. Without new elements introduced that change how the game is played, the horror side of the experience will degrade. Many games have attempted to spice things up by radically changing what is going on. In *Resident Evil 7*, the back half of the game takes place in two entirely different environments. Some titles may introduce new game systems to try and break up the core gameplay loop that was previously established. In *Bendy and the Ink Machine*, the game has several boss fights and arena battles to break up the slower adventure-styled gameplay (Figure 9.8).

Often, the problem with these approaches is that they are short-lived, and the game often returns to the status quo immediately after. When the horror of a title goes away, all that is left to keep the player engaged are the remaining elements: the story and the mechanics. Part of the reason for the decline in *Resident Evil*'s popularity was that by trying to experiment with more action-based design and ignoring the survival horror, the gameplay often proved to be too repetitive to keep the player engaged all the way through, or in the case of some of the spinoffs, the gameplay was not on par with other examples of the genre. This problem also occurred in *Alien Isolation*, with an estimated completion time around 15 hours, making it one of the longest horror games ever made. Without adding in new enemies, tricks by the Xenomorph, or options for the player, a common criticism was that the game grew repetitive.

One example I felt did things right in terms of pacing was *Yuppie Psycho* that I mentioned in the previous chapter. The game's length is about 7 hours give or take depending on what endings the player is trying to reach. For the game's final chapter, the entire environment gets changed after several major plot reveals, and the player is forced to adapt to finish the story.

The issues of pacing in a horror game are one of the reasons why microhorror (discussed last chapter) has become a solid alternative. The one problem is that it can leave the player with wanting more or feeling cheated if the game was too short or ended abruptly. Consumers these days are fine with paying more if the quality is there, but to a point. At the time of writing this book, the average price of indie games has gone up from $15 to between $20 and $25.

When it comes to progression in a horror game, it is important to look at what the player is doing and the obstacles in their way. In Section 4.4, I talked about world design when it comes to horror games. Thinking about your horror game as a set of sections is a good way to compartmentalize what it is like to play through it. When thinking about a section, you want each one to provide something different to keep the player invested. Often, each section has some larger goal that is preventing the player from moving on until its completed. For survival horror, it is typical to have a major roadblock that the player must find the ways to get around it via fighting, finding items, or solving puzzles.

Amnesia the Dark Descent was one of the first games to set up what would become a popular format for horror section design. Each area of the game had one major obstacle standing in the player's way. The solution to getting past it would also be broken up into different parts that were set up in several smaller sections nearby. Those sections were not connected to each other, and each one had a specific challenge or puzzle within them to complete.

In the *Resident Evil 2* remake, the player cannot move onto the second major area until they find three medallions, which the items needed to do that will take them across most of the police station. After getting them, the final obstacle is with the game's first boss fight. Even if you are designing your game around a chapter format, it is still important to consider the framing of each chapter. Each chapter in *Layers of Fear* is conceived as its own individual experience, complete from beginning to end. What you want to avoid is having chapters feel too like one another, leading to a sense of repetition.

An extremely popular structure is to reserve special enemies or situations as a chapter or section unto themselves. This can heighten the appearance of something new, provided that the same thing is not repeated later in the game. In *Amnesia the Dark Descent*, a section occurs early on that the player must dodge an invisible monster, with the only indication to their position are splashes in the water. To survive, the player must stay out of the water whenever possible to throw the monster off their position. With the *Resident Evil 2* remake, one of the hardest enemy types are monsters called "G-Adults," and they only show up specifically in the sewer section in the back half of the title (Figure 9.9). Structuring your game this way, clearing a difficult section, or getting around a special enemy can be a tension releasing moment as the player knows that it is now behind them.

Depending on the design, the layout of the game may require the player to return to previous areas. While this is an effective way of reusing content, it is important to give them a reason for doing so and throw something new at them. Whenever the player must return to an area in a *Resident Evil* title, there are usually new enemies to deal with that were not there previously. If the entire game space is open to the player, it becomes quite easy to get lost and frustrated. Many horror games would have locked doors and puzzles that the player would find early, and then get the item needed hours later. Without a way of notating this on a map, these games would turn into a scavenger hunt of trying to find the one door or remember where the puzzle was in the first place.

Microhorror, as I discussed last chapter, gets around the issues I have talked about here by the very fact that they are supposed to be a lean experience. With that said as the developer, you still need to approach your horror design understanding the pacing you want to get out of it. Even shorter games can still have

Figure 9.9

There are only a limited number of "G Adults" that show up during a single run of *Resident Evil 2*, but they are unpredictable, the largest common enemy, always fought in tight areas, and can waste a lot of resources if the player does not know how to get around them.

pacing issues and feel like they are being padded out: such as forcing the player to explore huge areas looking for items. Another mistake I see is when developers put something on a timer, and the only way to move forward is to literally wait for something to happen. I have often referred to this as "dead time," or when the player has no input on moving forward and just has to wait. Waiting for doors to open, loading animations, and slow walking animations, among other things, are distracting from your experience.

The last point regarding progression is about the power level of the player's character. Besides finding recovery items and ammo, you also need to decide whether the character will gain abilities or equipment that give them more power. Many survival and action horror games alike will reward players with weapons, more inventory space, new abilities, and more over the playthrough. These moments can either be joyous at the thought of the game getting easier or raise the tension as an indicator that something bad is about to happen that will require them. One of the oldest tricks in the book is to have the player fight tooth and nail to reach an important upgrade or key, and upon picking it up, trigger a boss fight or waves of enemies. While you want to give the player more power or new options to keep the game from growing repetitive, at the same time, if there is too much of a focus on growing in power, then the game turns into an action horror design.

Whether your game is 5 minutes or 5 hours long, your goal when designing and preparing the structure of your game is to make every minute worth it to the player's time. In section 9.6, I will be discussing the reason why frustration is the enemy of horror and something every developer needs to avoid.

9.5 Horror in Non-Horror Design

One of the more unique aspects to horror as a thematic genre is that it can show up even in properties that were not meant to be horror given the right conditions. Throughout this book, I have talked about horror along several lines: taking control away from the player, raising tension, and having the player face something that is unexpected. These elements are not exclusive to the horror genre and can often be used to great, or surprising, effect in other genres.

An infamous example that potentially scarred kids and parents alike came from the classic movie *Pee-wee's Big Adventure* in 1985 (Figure 9.10). In the scene, Pee-wee is talking to a trucker named Large Marge when she turns into a stop motion monster suddenly to deliver a jump scare. There is no other scene like this in the movie, and it completely comes out of nowhere to scare the audience.

In videogames, it is possible to put the player into a scary or tense situation by simply changing the tone or altering the gameplay. An extremely popular example of this has been used in many action games, where a specific section removes the player's ability to fight and forces them into sneaking around and avoiding detection. By subverting the core gameplay loop, you can put the player into a situation where they are forced to adapt and think on the fly. Returning to the *Thief* series, while the gameplay is balanced around the player being able

Figure 9.10

Anything that completely changes the tone of the story can become a potential point of horror, such as this shocking moment courtesy of Large Marge in *Pee-Wee's Big Adventure*.

to have an advantage in 1-on-1 fights, the earlier titles always had enemies built to mix things up. The first game introduced zombies that could not be killed by your regular weapons and had to be avoided or use holy water arrows or fire to kill them. In *Thief Deadly Shadows* (released in 2004), one level takes place in a destroyed orphanage; instead of fighting enemies, the player's mission is to find clues while being stalked by a ghost. Each game would have these sections where the player's traditional arsenal and tactics would not work, and they had to adapt.

Subverting what people expect to happen can be used for a quick sense of horror or to make a scene more striking. In *Undertale* developed by Toby Fox and released in 2015, a major aspect of the game was subverting what people know and expected out of RPGs. The first example of this was interacting with the character "Flowey" (Figure 9.11). Flowey appears throughout the game, and when you first talk to it, the character portrait looks happy and there is cheerful music playing. When the game wants to highlight something or accentuate a moment, the music would cut out and the portrait would change. Flowey would go through different portraits depending on the scene: happy, scared, sad, angry, and psychopathic.

Even games that are meant for younger fans or having a cartoon or fantasy aesthetic can have unexpected moments of horror. The game *A Hat in Time* released in 2017 by Gears for Breakfast was a 3D action platformer like the *Mario* series. Most of the core gameplay loop is about exploring levels looking for collectibles and completing objectives by jumping around. That changes for one specific level: Stage 3-4 Queen Vanessa's Manor (Figure 9.12). Instead of platforming, this level is about searching the manor for clues while the spirit of Vanessa stalks the player. The model for Vanessa is hazy, and the player never sees the full detail of it. When Vanessa is close, the screen starts to distort, the music becomes menacing, and the lighting becomes affected. The player's only defense

Figure 9.11

Flowey Omega completely clashes with the tone and aesthetic of *Undertale*, and changes the experience of playing the game.

Figure 9.12

A Hat in Time was pitched as a light-hearted adventure, and yet this scene comes completely out of nowhere to the point that it has scared people so hard that they stopped playing. Everything about the sound effects, camera angles, and the distortion is straight out of horror design.

is finding hiding spots and avoiding Vanessa's gaze. All the joyful aesthetics that are present in other levels is gone and replaced with much of the same horror tones I have spoken about in this book.

Understanding what can cause someone to be scared can be a useful skill when coming up with content in any medium. Adding just enough tension can elevate a scene or a section in a videogame and can leave a lasting impression on the consumer. Some of the most memorable parts of a videogame occur when something takes the player out of the normal experience and surprises them. With that said, it is important not to leave *too* much of a lasting impression. If you are designing something explicitly for kids, throwing in an intentionally over-the-top scary situation could lead to some angry parents.

9.6 Avoiding Frustration

Throughout this book, I have talked about the conditions needed for horror to work and how so much of it is focused on creating a specific experience for the player. While videogames are obviously an interactive medium compared to other products, this does present a problem when it comes to horror. The best examples of horror in other mediums do not require a lot of investment on the consumer's part – and the only interaction needed is to either read or watch. For videogames, interaction is required for someone to be able to experience the game, and if that interaction is terrible, then any attempt at horror is lost (Figure 9.13).

Every videogame needs to be play-tested to spot pain points in the design. This is where the concept of user interface and user experience (or UI/**UX**) design come in. One of the major problems that new developers have is understanding how to make their game as approachable as possible. **Approachability** transcends the aesthetic and design of your title, with the explicit goal to make your game as easy to play and get into as possible.

In Chapter 8, I talked about how horror has been kept alive by indie developers, but another reason why horror is niche is that many of the titles released are

Figure 9.13

Many indie developers will experiment with unique UIs and game mechanics that often lack the quality and refinement of established genres. It is also hard to tell from screenshots when there are issues, such as with Undiscovered here, and how the found footage aesthetic and camera view make the actual movement clunky.

behind the times in terms of UI/UX. There is a big difference between making a game that is challenging and making it challenging *to play the game.*

Over the course of the 2010s, I have played so many games whose UI is terrible and the basic experience of starting the game is frustrating. Here is a basic tip that designers say when it comes to design: The first part of your game should be the last part finished. A strong and easy to get into opening is often the difference between someone wanting to play your game or requesting a refund within minutes. As a developer, you do not have long to convince someone to play your game, and most people will decide within the first 30 minutes to an hour whether they want to keep going. It does not matter if your game improves in quality hours later if no one is staying around to see it.

When it comes specifically to the horror genre, there are many ways for the theme and gameplay of your title to suffer because of poor UI/UX, which in turn can ruin the experience. Back in Chapter 5, I talked about how any horror property only has one chance to make a good impression. Once frustration sets in about any part of your game, you have lost the player's interest and any tension is gone. It is a common issue among novice indie developers to make their UI hard to follow or annoying when trying to make their game challenging. It is extremely hard to scare someone when they are having trouble figuring out how your game works or is frustrated by the UI. Many horror titles are on the difficult side because of these annoyances, and this focus on difficulty has led to many games remaining niches.

Earlier in Section 6.5, I discussed puzzle design, and if a puzzle becomes too much of a focus or stops the player from proceeding, this can create a lot of frustration (Figure 9.14). In *The Beast Inside* (released in 2019 by Illusion Ray Studio), all progress in terms of the story and horror comes to a halt for a section where the

Figure 9.14

A frustrating puzzle is often the nail in the coffin for a lot of games, not just horror. This fuse puzzle from *Song of Horror* completely stopped me and I ended up quitting the game because of it.

player must use a code-breaking machine to move things along. The machine was annoying to use, and if the player makes one mistake, they must restart the entire process again. Some games will have a hint system that provides the player with guidance if they get stuck for too long. Another option seen in casual games is after an extended period of time being stuck at a puzzle, the game gives the player the option of just skipping the puzzle in order to keep the game moving along.

Another source of potential frustration is with the act of losing progress. Saving has become a standard functionality in games for years now. In horror games, being able to permanently lock in progress is also a tension release, and why there is a discussion about whether saving should be a part of the atmosphere. Some games let the player either save whenever they want or frequently autosave after progress has been made. Other titles will limit the ability to save by either only allowing it in certain areas, requiring a resource to be used, or both.

Losing progress and time is one of the most frustrating things that can happen in any videogame, and as the developer, it is something you need to consider when designing the gameplay of your title. Time is a valued commodity by everyone, and there are plenty of people who do not have the time to repeat minutes, or hours, of time lost. On the other hand, forcing the player into a section where they cannot just immediately restart like nothing happened can be a great source of tension and challenge. I do believe that every game should have the option to quick save the player's progress if they need to leave for whatever reason and then wipe the save when they load it back up.

The recent *Resident Evil* games struck a good balance in this regard. Playing on the lower difficulties, save points could be used infinitely. On the highest difficulty, the use of ink ribbons returned as a way of limiting saves. This was taken further by testing players to only save three times if they wanted the coveted S+ rank in the *Resident Evil 2* remake. It is better to let the player decide how much they want to save as opposed to forcing it upon them.

Some would argue that saving would not be needed with microhorror due to the experience being so short. However, losing progress no matter the length is still a major source of frustration. No one wants to repeat the exact thing they have already done due to losing at a later section. In *Game Design Deep Dives: Platformers*, I spoke about why platform designers will have checkpoints before and after difficult sections, as they want the player to only worry about the hard section and nothing else and reward them for finishing it. From a pacing perspective, try to avoid having something tedious or annoying before a difficult section that must be repeated on each attempt.

Beware of introducing difficulty spikes, or sections where the game immediately becomes far difficult than anything before. If the player is not prepared for it or lose a lot of progress because of it, there is a good chance they will stop playing and never come back. This can also occur if there are a fixed number of essential resources which the player drains constantly (Figure 9.15). In the *Outlast* series, the only way for the player to see in the dark is with the night vision mode of their camcorder. However, the camera is constantly draining batteries that must be

Figure 9.15

A common frustration point when the player must continually use limited consumable resources is that the longer it takes for them to solve an area, the worse off they will be. Since the world is handmade, there is only a finite number of consumables at any time. With the *Amnesia* series, running out of light sources will not only make it difficult to see what is happening, but punishes the player with screen distortions and sanity effects.

recharged, or the player becomes stuck in the dark. Running out of batteries and not being able to find anymore or reload a save to get more becomes a frustrating roadblock. A more practical option if you want to put a limit on an ability is to let the player use it as many times as they want but have a cooldown/recharge period on extended use. This way, the item must still be managed, but they are not punished in the future for repeated use in the present. For games that allow the player to sprint, this is the exact mechanic used when balancing a "run bar" or stamina gauge.

This section of this book is universal to every genre, and a developer who does not think about UI/UX will always struggle to get consumers to look at their game. Good horror often does a lot with little in terms of mechanics, and no matter how big or small your game systems are, they should be enjoyable to play.

10

The Future of Horror

Figure 10.1

While writing this book, *Resident Evil Village* was released to critical and commercial success. At this time, there are rumors of AAA horror games in the works, but nothing for certain.

DOI: 10.1201/9781003199250-10

10.1 Is There a Market for Horror?

For the final chapter, I want to hypothesize about what horror means in the coming decade and beyond for the game industry. Despite successes like the recent *Resident Evil* games, or the concept of microhorror with the *Dread X* collections, horror is not in the same place it was 20 years ago (Figure 10.1). Many games from the indie space that have been considered successes still only have a few thousand reviews, which does not make for a far-reaching game. Exceptions like *Amnesia*, *Five Night's at Freddy's*, and *Outlast* are still around, but their later entries are not as popular as the first ones.

And that takes me to the question posed for this section: Is the industry heading for a resurgence of mainstream horror, or is this simply a quick bump followed by a downturn? At this moment, I feel that horror as a viable genre has a chance. In the past 4 years, the expectations and quality from the indie space has grown, and it is giving developers the opportunity to focus on making amazing games worth every dollar. With that said, this does not mean to simply recreate games from the early 2000s in terms of aesthetics and gameplay. Nor does this mean to keep borrowing from the same playbook that titles like *Amnesia* and *Outlast* created.

There are plenty of amazing concepts for horror that have come from smaller developers, but I have personally not seen one that has managed to revolutionize horror for audiences in the same way that *Resident Evil* has done now arguably three times over with *Resident Evil*, *Resident Evil 4*, and *Resident Evil 7*. You may be thinking it is not fair to compare indie developers to similar standards, but there have been indie games who have managed to sell more in their respective genres than major companies and have had massive success.

At the time of writing this book, many indie developers are now creating games with the look and aesthetics of early 3D/PlayStation 2 era titles (as I discussed in Chapter 8), and unfortunately that is not what I am talking about in terms of elevating the genre. Many developers are using nostalgia as a selling point, especially for horror games due to the as-for-mentioned AAA crash back in Chapter 7. However, just making games that look and feel like something from 20 years ago is not moving the market forward, and these developers tend to fall into traps when it comes to onboarding.

In Section 9.6, I spoke about avoiding frustration and the importance of play-testing and approachability, and I feel this is where indie horror developers need to focus on if they are hoping to break out. It is hard to recommend a lot of the indie horror games to people who are not familiar in that space due to the issues when it comes to approachability. There is room today for someone to approach a horror game with the same passion and growth that I have seen from the growth of roguelike design, and something I want to elaborate on in the next section.

With that said, I do have a warning for both indie and AAA companies alike. As I have spoken at length about in this book, Horror as a genre is not like any other in the game industry. The absolute best all-around amazing examples of it still pale in terms of sales and consumer base compared to other genres. A lot of what makes horror work is not about expensive production values, hiring big name voice talent, or using the best game engines on the market, but focusing on the psychological elements throughout this book. Anyone who is expecting a horror game today to pull in tens of millions of copies sold is deluding themselves. According to financial reports released by Capcom, *Resident Evil 7* has sold 8.5 million copies across all platforms and the *Resident Evil 2* remake 7.8 million copies as of December 31, 2020,[1] and those would be considered the current tops when it comes to horror videogames today. As a quick aside, part of the reason for these larger numbers was also the fact that Capcom is releasing their games on more platforms as cross-launches and is tabulating the sales as one version instead of multiple. Still, those are very impressive numbers for horror games to pull in and beat the best examples released during the survival horror heyday.

And even with that success, both of those titles still suffer from much of the same issues that have plagued horror for decades in terms of pacing. There is one avenue that still has not been explored by horror design fully, and it takes me to one of my dream ideas.

10.2 Procedurally Generated Horror

Section 8.3 I briefly spoke about how more developers are using procedural generation in their games, which has led to a growing adoption of roguelike elements and design these days. For many horror titles, they have used procedural generation in terms of map layouts and item placements which shuffles up the experience but does not change it on a run-by-run basis.

Where I personally feel horror has yet to go is delivering a full-on horror roguelike, a game where the environments, enemies, events, and challenges are different each time. In the same section, I briefly mentioned *World of Horror* which is one of the more forward-thinking horror games I have played with its roguelike elements (Figure 10.2). However, I would argue that it is still too limited at this time in terms of pacing and elements to provide enough **variance** for a roguelike. For now, a closer example would be the game *Golden Light* being developed by Mr. Pink (Figure 10.3). Levels are procedurally generated along with what items and artifacts are found on each play. The game is played mostly in the dark with a low field of view to make things oppressive like *Lost in Vivo*. Instead of just having different enemies, many of them are always disguised as inanimate objects that litter the area who spring up to attack when the player gets too close.

Throughout this book, I have described good horror design as a carefully curated experience, and it is easy to assume that procedural generation would upset horror due to the randomness and unpredictability it creates, but that is exactly why it can improve horror design. Good procedural generation is not about making chaos but creating a new experience each time to keep the player guessing. In Chapter 4, I spoke about how true horror is about the unknown and

---

[1] https://www.capcom.co.jp/ir/english/finance/million.html.

Figure 10.2

A scene from World of Horror showing the event "Bad Feeling" and the threat level increasing.

Figure 10.3

Golden Light is an example of a game that make great use of an oppressive atmosphere, combined with the roguelike elements, to keep the player always unsure about what's going to happen next.

trying to deal with it. When I talked about pacing issues in the last chapter, they stem from the horror design becoming repetitive. The absolute best horror games released in the last 30 years can only be experienced fresh one time.

What I envision is a horror game that has a pool of different enemies, major and minor events, and possible areas that will appear, and the game will use that to create a unique playthrough on each run. The player has a rough idea from playing the game as to what to expect from a core gameplay loop perspective, but they will not know what is out to get them until they stumble upon it during play. This kind of approach also creates a modular kind of design that can be expanding with new elements which also solves the problem of trying to keep creating content for a horror experience. Incidentally, this methodology is also being applied to *World of Horror* in how its events and run structure work.

As I said, many horror games already use procedural generation in small ways to keep the player guessing, and my idea is to take that even further.

10.3 Summary

Not many people think about horror design beyond jump scares and lots of blood, but there is a huge difference in quality throughout the many kinds of horror seen. This is a genre that if you do it right, it means that less people will probably want to check out a game that is going to terrify them. From the cheesy, to the horrific, to the cute, to the psychological, there is a huge pool to drawn on when designing your game (Figure 10.4).

Regardless of what kind of design you are aiming for, be careful when trying to copy another game's style or horror, as repetition is the enemy of horror. Being able to create something that can elicit an emotional response is a work of art. Even if you are not interested in terrifying someone, the lessons learned can help you when it comes to making a memorable and tense scene.

Looking back on writing the previous *Game Design Deep Dive*, I still find it fascinating with how far the indie scene has taken platformer, roguelike, and now horror compared to larger companies. The 2010s was the decade of indie development coming into its own, and the 2020s I feel will be one of the most creative decades of game development and is the time for horror to come back with new designs.

Thank you for picking up this book and letting me finally get out all my thoughts on the horror genre in one place. If you have any questions or just want to share your comments, you can find my contact information under the social media contact section.

Figure 10.4

I'm afraid our time is over. Thank you for reading this book. As one last indie horror recommendation, check out House for a *Groundhog Day*-inspired experience.

Glossary

AAA: Shorthand for a major studio or publisher in the game industry.

Alpha Antagonist: Used to describe an enemy that is actively chasing after the player and cannot be permanently stopped.

Approachability: How easy is it for someone to start enjoying your game regardless of their skill level.

Asymmetrical Balance: Designing a game where each participant has their own unique abilities and options instead of everyone playing the same way.

Core Gameplay Loop: The primary game system that a player will be making use of the most when playing a videogame.

Customization: Game systems that allow the player to alter their character and change what they can do gameplaywise.

Diegetic: For videogames, this is when elements like the UI and music exist within the game space as opposed to just being there for the player's benefit. A simple example would be having radios that play music instead of it just existing everywhere the player goes.

Dynamic: The interaction between two different game systems that creates an interesting link between the two.

ESRB: Stands for "Entertainment Software Rating Board" organization that officially rates games in the United States in terms of content, much like the rating system for movies.

Event Triggers: A conditional based off the player-controlled character performing a specific action and the game reacting a certain way because of it.

First-Person: A camera style and game genre that positions the camera as if the player is looking directly out of the eyes of the character.

FMV: Stands for "full motion video," a term used for when games use real people behind digitized, or computer generated, sets. All footage used is recorded, as opposed to animating game characters.

GDC: Stands for "Game Developers Conference," an annual tradeshow focusing on game development and panels by game developers.

Gunplay: Used to describe the overall feel of a weapon in either a first- or third-person shooter.

Indie: Also referred to as an indie developer, someone who creates games without the need of a large studio and major investors.

IP: Stands for "Intellectual Property" and is referenced here for games that use someone else's creative work for their game.

Jump Scare: A sudden audio or visual trick used to shock and scare the player made famous by horror games.

Lore: Used to describe the history of the events that happened in a story that are not related to the plot or main character.

Mechanics: The actions or "verbs" that someone will make use of while playing a videogame.

Microtransactions: The act of selling smaller purchases inside a videogame. Popularized by mobile games, but can be seen in larger titles, to buy new cosmetics or in-game advantages.

NPC: Stands for non-playable character and refers to any characters in a game that are not controlled by a player.

Player: The person who is playing the videogame.

PEGI: Stands for "Pan European Game Information," an organization that rates games and assigns them a rating in terms of content for games released in the European markets.

Permadeath: Games that delete the player's save file if they die and require them to restart from the beginning. Also referred to as "hardcore mode" or "ironman difficulty."

Port: When a game is released on different platforms than the one it was designed primarily for. The two big examples are going from a PC to a console and vice versa.

Procedural Generation: Having the game generate content while the game is running, often used to create items or new game spaces and has been featured heavily in roguelike design.

Power Curve: An abstract way to define how strong a character becomes over the length of a game and how it relates to progression.

Quick Time Event: Also known as a "QTE." A situation where the player must quickly press the corresponding button or make a decision before something bad happens.

Respawn: When something is revived in a game after being either killed or used (if it is an item).

Role Playing Game: Also known as "RPG," refers to games that focus on in-game characters becoming stronger as opposed to the player's own skill and hand–eye coordination.

ROM: Stands for "read only memory," and for videogames references an image of the software that can be emulated without the need of the original copy or hardware. Creating a rom of a videogame and emulating it is a practice that is currently considered illegal.

Roguelike: A game genre that focuses on someone replaying it and getting a difference experience each time.

Soft Lock: When the player reaches a point where they are unable to continue playing a game due to technical or gameplay issues, but the game is not crashing and is still technically working.

Soulslike: A term popularized by the *Dark Souls* series by From Software and corresponds to games that mirror the design and structure of it.

Speedrunning: Describing playing a game with the intent of finishing it in the fastest way possible.

System: A way of categorizing related mechanics and organizing them.

Top-Down: A camera style used in videogames that shows the game space as if the player is looking directly down from the sky at the action.

UI: Short for user interface and represents all the ways the player will interact with the game and be given information by the game.

UX: Short for user experience and is a way of examining the difficulty of how someone interacts with the game.

Variance: The ways in which the mechanics or content generation in a game can provide the player with a unique experience on each play.

Index

Note: *Italic* page numbers refer to figures.

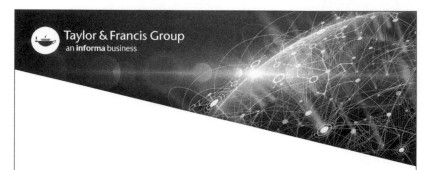